HOME AT SEVEN

A play in three acts

by R.C. Sherriff

samuelfrench.co.uk

Copyright © 1950 by R.C. Sherriff

HOME AT SEVEN is fully protected under the copyright laws of the British Commonwealth, including Canada, the United States of America, and all other countries of the Copyright Union. All rights, including professional and amateur stage productions, recitation, lecturing, public reading, motion picture, radio broadcasting, television and the rights of translation into foreign languages are strictly reserved.

ISBN 978-0-573-01185-6

www.samuelfrench.co.uk
www.samuelfrench.com

For Amateur Production Enquiries

United Kingdom and World excluding North America

plays@samuelfrench.co.uk
020 7255 4302/01

Each title is subject to availability from Samuel French, depending upon country of performance.

CAUTION: Professional and amateur producers are hereby warned that HOME AT SEVEN is subject to a licensing fee. Publication of this play does not imply availability for performance. Both amateurs and professionals considering a production are strongly advised to apply to the appropriate agent before starting rehearsals, advertising, or booking a theatre. A licensing fee must be paid whether the title is presented for charity or gain and whether or not admission is charged.

The professional rights in this play are controlled by Samuel French Ltd, 24-32 Stephenson Way, London NW1 2HD.

No one shall make any changes in this title for the purpose of production. No part of this book may be reproduced, stored in a retrieval system, or transmitted in any form, by any means, now known or yet to be invented, including mechanical, electronic, photocopying, recording, videotaping, or otherwise, without the prior written permission of the publisher. No one shall upload this title, or part of this title, to any social media websites.

The right of R.C. Sherriff to be identified as author of this work has been asserted in accordance with Section 77 of the Copyright, Designs and Patents Act 1988.

HOME AT SEVEN

Produced at Wyndham's Theatre, London, on March 7th, 1950, with the following cast of characters:

(in the order of their appearance)

MRS PRESTON	*Marian Spencer.*
DAVID PRESTON	*Ralph Richardson.*
DR SPARLING	*Cyril Raymond.*
MAJOR WATSON	*Philip Stainton.*
INSPECTOR HEMINGWAY	*Campbell Singer.*
MR PETHERBRIDGE, a Solicitor	*Frederick Piper.*
PEGGY DOBSON	*Meriel Forbes.*

SYNOPSIS OF SCENES

The action of the play passes in the sitting-room of David Preston's home at Bromley, Kent.

TIME.—Autumn in the present year.

ACT I

SCENE 1.—Seven o'clock on a Tuesday evening.
SCENE 2.—Half an hour later.

ACT II

SCENE 1.—Nine o'clock the next morning.
SCENE 2.—Half an hour later.

ACT III

Towards seven o'clock the following evening.

To face page 1.—Home at Seven

HOME AT SEVEN

ACT I

Scene 1

Scene.—*The sitting-room of* David Preston's *home at Bromley, Kent. Seven o'clock on a Tuesday evening. Autumn of the present year.*

The house is a small semi-detached one in a quiet road of similar houses, and the sitting-room has the comfortable appearance of belonging to homely people. The door is up C. *and leads into a small entrance hall with access to the kitchen and stairs to the bedrooms. There are french windows* C. *of a large bay up* L. *They are flanked by the ordinary type of sliding windows. The french windows open on to a conservatory where there are shelves with a display of dwarf chrysanthemums in pots. Through the window* R. *of the french windows can be seen the porch with an outer glass-panelled door to it. This window is open slightly so that conversation in the porch can be heard. The front door proper is* L. *of the entrance hall. The path down the front garden can be seen through the glass of the conservatory and passes to* L. *above it, with the gate at the* L. *end, so that anyone approaching the front door can be seen. A nearby lamp-post throws a little light around the gate when it is dark. The entrance hall is furnished with a grandfather clock, coat-rack and umbrella stand. The conservatory is furnished with a wicker table and chair. In the room the fireplace is* C. *of the wall* R. *The curtains and carpets are good without being expensive; tasteful without being inspired. A cretonne-covered comfortable three-piece suite stands* R., *the sofa at right angles to the fire, one easy chair below the fire and the other* C., *facing down* R. *A low coffee table stands below the sofa, an occasional table with a table-lamp on it below the fire, and another occasional table with a vase of flowers on it stands* R. *of the door up* C. *In the corner up* R. *there is a table on which stands a wireless receiver. A writing-desk with an armchair to it stands in the bay. A long fireside stool stands* R. *of the desk. Two dining chairs stand* R. *and* L. *of the bay. There is a small bookcase against the wall down* L., *and a low armchair down* L. *completes the furnishing. The floor, entrance hall and stairs are carpeted. At night the room is lit by electric-candle wall-brackets* R. *and* L. *of the fireplace and* R. *and* L. *of the bay, and a standard lamp above the* R. *end of the sofa. A light with a "lantern" shade hangs in the porch. A couple of*

good *prints hang on the walls, and there is a large mirror over the mantelpiece.*
(*See the Ground Plan and Photograph of the Scene.*)

When the CURTAIN *rises it is early evening and still light outside, but growing darker as the scene is played. The lights in the room have not yet been lit, nor the curtains drawn. A cheerful fire burns in the grate. A tray of tea has been set on the coffee stool. The telephone has been lifted off the desk and stands prominently on the upstage end of the stool* R. *of the desk.* MRS JANET PRESTON *is seated in the firelight at the* L. *end of the sofa. She has a rug across her knees. She is a quiet, good-looking woman of forty. She dresses well in the sense that one does not really notice what she wears, and her greying hair is simply, almost austerely arranged. She may have been a clergyman's daughter or school-teacher before she married. She is sitting forward, with a twisted sodden handkerchief in her hand. Now and then she sobs, dejectedly and hopelessly, as if she has cried so much that her tears are dry and her misery exhausted. She is pale and haggard, and her eyes are dark from sleeplessness. After a few moments, she rises, crosses to the french windows and without opening them, looks towards the gate and street, then moves to the coffee table, picks up the tray of tea and exits with it up* C. *to the kitchen, leaving the door wide open. Presently,* DAVID PRESTON *appears at the gate, passes briskly into the porch, opens the front door with his key, and comes into the entrance hall. As he enters the house the clock strikes seven.* PRESTON *wears his overcoat and a bowler hat, and carries a neatly furled umbrella and an evening paper. He is a tall, well-built man of fifty, smartly dressed in the dark jacket and grey-striped trousers of a well-placed city man. He looks, in fact, what he is—a senior official in a London Bank. He is obviously quite unaware of his wife's distress because he hums a cheerful tune as he hangs up his hat and coat, puts his umbrella in the stand, and enters the room. He walks in like any other normal city man returning from the office in the evening, tired from a day's work and eager for a cup of tea and the comfort of his fireside. He drops the paper on the coffee table, moves below the sofa to* R. *of it, leans over and switches on the standard lamp. As he does so,* MRS PRESTON *enters up* C.

MR PRESTON (*moving below the coffee table*). Hullo, my dear. (*He throws a casual, friendly glance at* MRS PRESTON, *so casual that he does not notice her distress, then looks in surprise at the empty coffee table*). Why—where's my cup of tea?

(*He glances back enquiringly at her, and his home-coming brightness suddenly becomes concern as* MRS PRESTON *moves unsteadily, pitifully in to* L. *of him, and throws herself into his arms.*)

MRS PRESTON. Oh, David! My darling—my darling. (*She clings to him, sobbing her heart out.*)
MR PRESTON (*astonished*). Janet! What on earth's the matter? What's happened?
(*She does not answer. All her pent-up anxiety and torment comes streaming out in a flood of tears.* MR PRESTON *is bewildered.*)
What is it, Janet? Aren't you well? For heaven's sake, please! What is it?
MRS PRESTON. Oh, David—it's been terrible. I didn't know what to do. What happened to you? Where have you been?
MR PRESTON (*blankly*). Where have I been? To the office, of course. Where d'you think I've been?
MRS PRESTON. But last night—and all today?

(MR PRESTON *stares at her, completely at a loss. Then he gently takes her arm and leads her to the easy chair* C. *where she sits. He is frightened now, and speaks to her gently and soothingly.*)

MR PRESTON. I've never seen you like this before. I'll get you a cup of tea. (*He pauses and moves to* L. *of the coffee table.*) If you didn't feel well, why didn't you ring me at the Bank? You only had to phone, and I'd have come home at once.

(MRS PRESTON *grows calmer. She looks at him in a strange perplexity.*)

MRS PRESTON. I've been in torment all day and all last night. I thought I was going mad.
MR PRESTON. All last night? What do you mean, dear—all last night?
MRS PRESTON. When you didn't come home.
MR PRESTON (*trying to soothe her; gently*). Janet, dear (*he moves to the fireplace and indicates the clock*) look at the clock up there. It's just gone seven. I'm always home at this time—every night. There's nothing for you to be anxious about. It's been just an ordinary day, dear—just like any other Monday.
MRS PRESTON. But today's Tuesday.
MR PRESTON (*with a slight laugh*). Monday, darling.
MRS PRESTON (*obstinately*). It's Tuesday, David.
MR PRESTON (*still trying to soothe her; anxiously*). You're tired, Janet. You've got confused. I *do* know what day of the week it is. Yesterday was Sunday. Don't you remember? It rained a little in the morning but it cleared up before we went to church. (*He picks up the rug off the sofa and folds it.*) In the afternoon we worked in the garden. You pruned the rose trees and I cut the lawn. After supper we listened to the radio —you remember—the serial—that Jane Austen story.

(*There is a pause.* MRS PRESTON *is quite calm now.*)

(*He puts the rug over the* L. *end of the sofa.*) I'll just go and make you a cup of tea, dear. (*He moves to her and pats her hand.*) You probably had an afternoon nap and *dreamed* that I didn't come home. (*He smiles.*) But I did, and everything's all right. (*He moves to the door up* C.)

MRS PRESTON (*rising suddenly*). David. Just a moment. (*She picks up the paper from the coffee table, glances at it, without surprise, and turns to him.*) The evening paper you brought in. Look—Tuesday.

(MR PRESTON *moves to* L. *of her, takes the paper and looks blankly at the date on it.*)

MR PRESTON. That's extraordinary. They—they don't often make mistakes like that. They must have given me the wrong paper.

MRS PRESTON. Then you'd better look at this morning's paper.

MR PRESTON (*putting the evening paper on the coffee table*). The morning paper isn't here because I took it with me to the office. You *know* I always take it with me, Janet.

MRS PRESTON (*crossing to the stool*). You didn't take the morning paper because you weren't here to take it. (*She picks up " The Times " and " Amateur Gardening " from the stool, glances at them and moves to* L. *of* MR PRESTON. *She reads.*) " Tuesday the twenty-seventh." (*She holds the paper out to him.*) You see?

(MR PRESTON *takes the paper and stares at the date. At first he does not even begin to understand the significance of it.*)

(*She holds up " Amateur Gardening ".*) And here's *Amateur Gardening* that always comes—every Tuesday. (*She drops it back on to the stool.*)

(MR PRESTON *moves to the fireplace and looks again at the date on the paper.*)

(*She speaks now very calmly. There is sorrow in her voice but no rebuke or anger. If she feels any anger, she firmly conceals it.*) We've always (*she moves quickly to* L. *of the sofa*) understood one another so perfectly, David. If you suddenly felt you wanted to go away and be alone for a while, well, that's perfectly all right. I should have understood. Why couldn't you have telephoned and *told* me you weren't coming home?

(MR PRESTON *has only partly heard what she has said. He is too bewildered and too frightened to understand. He turns, drops the paper on to the coffee table and answers her as quietly as she has spoken to him, but he gropes uncertainly, struggling for a clue to the mystery.*)

Mr Preston. Something I—I don't understand has happened, Janet. (*He switches on the table-lamp down* R.) You must give me time to think because I—I'm sure there's really quite a simple explanation, that'll come in a minute. (*He stands with his back to the fire.*) Anybody at the Bank could tell you I've been there all day.

Mrs Preston (*moving below the* L. *end of the sofa*). You've not been at the Bank all day—I rang the Manager.

Mr Preston. But I have, Janet.

(*There is a pause.* Mrs Preston *has listened patiently—without believing a word. She begins, quietly and deliberately, to tell him her own story.*)

Mrs Preston. I had your tea ready on this table here at seven o'clock last night, like I always do. When you didn't come in I thought you had missed your train at Cannon Street —or perhaps it was late for some reason. Then eight o'clock came. (*She turns, moves above the stool and looks towards the window.*) I was terribly worried because you always telephone me if you're going to be late. I thought you must have had an accident. (*She turns.*) I went in to the Warrens next door although I scarcely know them. Mr Warren said the trains were running quite normally and he suggested ringing up the Bank. He rang up for me, but there was only a cleaner there. (*She moves* C.) Then he said you might have come in while I was at his house, so I came back, but you weren't here, and it was nearly nine o'clock. I was so terribly anxious—(*she glances at the telephone, then back to* Mr Preston) and then I rang up the police.

Mr Preston (*appalled*). You rang up the *police!*

Mrs Preston (*moving to* L. *of the sofa; with her first flash of anger*). What did you expect me to do? Did you expect me to lock up the house and go to bed as if nothing had happened?

(*There is a pause.* Mr Preston *sits in the easy chair down* R.)

(*She resumes in her calm, deliberate voice again.*) The Sergeant on duty said he would enquire at the hospitals and let me know if anyone had been brought in. Later he rang up to say they couldn't trace anyone who might be you. (*She perches herself on the* L. *arm of the sofa.*) I sat up in this chair all night—waiting and listening. When the Bank was open I rang up the Manager. He said you hadn't come in this morning—but you left the previous night *as usual* at five o'clock. (*She looks at him.*) You say you left at six, David. You told me you always leave at six.

Mr Preston (*uncomfortably*). That's right, Janet. I always do. At six.

Mrs Preston. I asked him again because it surprised me. He repeated it. He said you always leave at five.

MR PRESTON (*rising and moving to the fireplace*). He must have made a mistake—(*he stands half-turned from her*) or you misunderstood him. *He always leaves at five.* (*He turns.*) He was speaking of himself when he said that.

(*There is a pause.* MRS PRESTON *decides to let this pass, but gradually her manner hardens. She is convinced now that he is deceiving her.*)

MRS PRESTON. About noon, he rang again and said you still hadn't come in. Since then I've just sat here—for hours and hours, and I thought I was going mad. (*She rises.*) And then you walk in, David, as if nothing had happened, and say I dreamed it all. (*She moves to the easy chair* C. *and shakes up the cushions.*)

MR PRESTON. I can only tell you one thing, Janet. Unless I've taken leave of my senses, I've been at the Bank all day, and done the usual work I always do on Monday. Look at my clothes. Do I *look* as if I've wandered about all night ? (*He glances at his hands, turns and looks in the mirror over the mantelpiece.*) Where could I have washed and shaved ? (*He runs his hand over his chin.*) Do I look any different from what I look when I come in every evening from the office ? (*He turns.*) Coming down the road just now I was thinking of the ordinary, everyday things I always think about on my way home—the tulips to put in round the house next Sunday ; the accounts of the Social Club to get ready for the general meeting next month ; our evening at the pictures on Thursday. (*He pauses, then shakes his head.*) You're angry when I said you must have dozed and dreamed it, Janet. But what else *can* I think ? (*He glances at the papers on the coffee table.*) These papers—(*he bends over and touches them for a moment*) I—I don't understand. But there *must* be some explanation——

(*The telephone rings. They both start nervously.*)

—some quite simple explanation. (*His words trail uncertainly away. His effort to convince himself has not been altogether satisfactory.*)

(MRS PRESTON *moves to the stool, transfers the telephone on to the upstage end of the desk, switches on the desk-lamp, then lifts the telephone receiver.*)

MRS PRESTON (*into the telephone*). Hullo ? . . . Yes. It's Mrs Preston speaking . . . Good evening, Mr Cooper . . .

(MR PRESTON *moves* C.)

Yes. He's just come in . . . Yes. I see . . . No, he's—he's quite all right . . . I don't know . . . Yes. I'll tell him. (*She covers the mouthpiece of the telephone with her hand and turns* to MR PRESTON.) It's the Bank Manager. (*She holds the receiver out to* MR PRESTON.) He says you haven't been at the Bank all day. He'd like to speak to you. (*She hands the receiver to him, turns to the window up* L.C. *and draws the curtain.*)

(MR PRESTON *hesitates a moment before speaking.*)

MR PRESTON (*into the telephone*). Good evening, Mr Cooper, sir . . .

(MRS PRESTON *draws the curtain across the french windows.*)

Yes, I'm quite all right . . . I don't know . . . I'd—I'd like to talk to you . . .

(MRS PRESTON *draws the curtain across the window* L.)

I—I really can't tell you anything now. I'll—I'll be at the Bank early—at a quarter to nine—and come and see you in your office . . . Good night, sir. (*He replaces the receiver, looking dazed and frightened. With scarcely a glance at* MRS PRESTON *he sits at the desk and stares ahead of him.*)

(MRS PRESTON *watches him. She is torn by uncertainty. She does not know what to think, but uppermost in her mind is the belief that he is concealing something from her.*)

MRS PRESTON (*after a pause*). I expect you'd like me to get you a cup of tea.

She crosses to the door up C. *as—*

the CURTAIN *falls.*

SCENE 2

SCENE.—*The same. Half an hour later.*

When the CURTAIN *rises the room is empty. The window curtains are still closed and the wall-brackets are on so that the room is brightly lit.* MRS PRESTON *is in the entrance hall with* DR SPARLING, *who has just arrived at the house. He is a good, normal General Practitioner; a simple man who does not believe in behaving too much like a doctor. He is about the same age as* MR PRESTON, *and is honest, friendly and sensible. He carries a small medical bag. He puts his hat on the coat-rack and enters the room, followed by* MRS PRESTON *who closes the door behind her.*

MRS PRESTON. My husband's upstairs lying down. I'll tell him you're here, Doctor.

DOCTOR (*moving down* L.C.). I'll go up if you like.

MRS PRESTON (*moving* C.). I think he'd rather see you down

here. He never likes to think he's ill. He didn't want me to call you but I think you ought to see him.

DOCTOR (*putting his bag on the stool*). Have you noticed anything—*unusual* about him lately?

MRS PRESTON. Nothing. He's been a little worried about one or two things, but perfectly all right in himself.

DOCTOR. You definitely think he's ill?

MRS PRESTON. I don't know. I know nothing more than what I told you on the phone. He came in looking quite well and cheerful. He looked perfectly all right, until I told him what had happened. Then—well—he refused to believe it until I showed him the paper, and the Bank Manager rang up.

DOCTOR. He believed it then?

MRS PRESTON. Naturally. He *had* to believe it. What else *could* he do?

DOCTOR. He couldn't possibly have thought he could walk in like that and make you believe that nothing had happened —unless he honestly believed that nothing had happened himself.

MRS PRESTON. I know. That's what I don't understand. He's such an honest man, Doctor. I don't think he's ever told a lie in his life. I believe he was absolutely genuine when he seemed surprised, and yet—I had a feeling he was concealing something.

DOCTOR. Oh!

MRS PRESTON (*leaning on the back of the easy chair* C.). Well, it's a small thing. He told me he left his office at six o'clock last night—he *always* says he leaves at six. But the Manager told me on the phone that he leaves at five—regularly—every night.

DOCTOR. Well, that hardly explains him being away for twenty-four hours. (*He pauses.*) Did you ask him about it— about the time of his leaving?

MRS PRESTON. Yes. He said it was a mistake. He definitely said he leaves at six. He said I must have misunderstood the Manager. He was so certain that I *must* believe him.

DOCTOR (*nodding*). Of course.

MRS PRESTON. You don't know us very well, Doctor, because we're hardly ever ill. But I think you ought to know that we're absolutely happy together.

DOCTOR. I'm sure of that. (*He smiles.*)

MRS PRESTON. And that made it rather hard for me to tell him. (*She hesitates.*) But I did try to make him realize that I would understand perfectly if he wanted to go off by himself for a while.

DOCTOR. What did he say?

MRS PRESTON. He said quite definitely that there was nothing. Absolutely nothing. He swore that he was telling me the truth.

(*There is a slight pause.*)

DOCTOR. Then I think you should accept that.
MRS PRESTON. I do. Because I'm certain he always *has* told me the truth—in all the years we've been together.

(*The* DOCTOR *nods. There is a short silence. Then he becomes brisk and professional.*)

DOCTOR. Well, then. If you'll tell him I'm here . . .
MRS PRESTON. Yes. (*She moves towards the door up* C.)
DOCTOR. You say he didn't want to see me?
MRS PRESTON. Only because he hates the idea of being ill —but I—I think he was glad when I insisted.

(*The* DOCTOR *nods.*)

Will you want him to take anything off?
DOCTOR. Oh no. I don't think so.
MRS PRESTON (*picking up the rug from the sofa arm*). Then it won't be necessary to make the fire up. (*She opens the door up* C. *and calls up the stairs.*) David, Dr Sparling's come.
MR PRESTON (*off upstairs; calling*). I'm coming.

(MRS PRESTON *exits to the kitchen. She takes the rug with her and closes the door behind her. The* DOCTOR *moves to the fireplace and waits. He makes no pretensions about being a psychiatrist. He has never, probably, had a case like this before and is not altogether comfortable about it. After a few moments,* MR PRESTON *enters up* C. *He looks pale and drawn, but tries to conceal his anxiety. He has put on a lounge jacket, but otherwise he is in the clothes he came home in. He leaves the door up* C. *ajar.*)

DOCTOR (*holding out his hand; with a cheerful smile*). Good evening.
MR PRESTON (*moving to* L. *of the* DOCTOR). Good evening, Doctor.

(*They shake hands.*)

DOCTOR. Well—it's quite a while since we last met.

(*Both men make conversation for their own different purposes. The* DOCTOR *to set his patient at ease, and to test his memory:* MR PRESTON *to show the* DOCTOR *that he is quite normal. But neither is really comfortable:* MR PRESTON *is trying hard to appear composed—but he is nervous, puzzled and frightened.*)

MR PRESTON. Yes. That knee of mine—two years ago now.
DOCTOR. Has it been all right?
MR PRESTON. Perfectly. I rubbed that liniment in a couple of times and forgot all about it.
DOCTOR. Good. We've met since then. D'you remember— the Social Club dance?

MR PRESTON (*nodding*). At Christmas. Yes, we had quite a good crowd that evening.

DOCTOR. A lot of young people, I noticed.

MR PRESTON. We encourage the young ones all we can. Clubs have a way of getting old before their time—so we make a rule to elect at least three " under-twenties " to the Committee every year.

DOCTOR. Good idea. Keeps you pretty busy—Treasurer of a big Club like that?

MR PRESTON. It does rather: takes a good deal of time—but I enjoy it.

DOCTOR. How many members have you got?

MR PRESTON. Oh—well over three hundred this year.

DOCTOR. It's a big thing.

MR PRESTON. It is now. I helped to start it ten years ago. We began with fifteen members. We've gone ahead fast these past few years.

(*There is a pause.*)

DOCTOR. Well! Shall we . . . You're *looking* very well.

MR PRESTON (*sitting in the easy chair* C.). I *feel* well. Perfectly well. (*He pauses.*) My wife told you on the phone what happened?

DOCTOR (*standing below the coffee table*). Yes. She told me everything you had told her. As a matter of fact I knew last night that—er—something had happened.

MR PRESTON (*sharply*). How?

DOCTOR. The police rang through to the hospital to ask if anyone had been brought in. I was there at the time. They gave your name of course, and knowing you as most of us did, we were naturally concerned.

MR PRESTON. I'm sorry my wife did that.

DOCTOR. I think she did the only thing possible in the circumstances.

MR PRESTON. Oh, quite. I realize that. But you know, one doesn't want a lot of talk.

DOCTOR. Of course—but I don't think you need worry. Have you let the police know you're home?

MR PRESTON. Yes. My wife called up and told them.

DOCTOR. Well—that's all right then. (*He pauses.*) I understand from your wife that you left for the City in the usual way yesterday morning. You came home this evening at your usual time—believing it was the same day—when it was actually a day later?

MR PRESTON. Yes. (*He pauses.*) It's all so queer, Doctor. I got home as I always do—just at seven. I was feeling perfectly all right. I found my wife in a terrible state. When she told me what had happened I thought she must have dreamt it. I couldn't believe it until I saw the date on the newspapers —and the Bank Manager rang up and said I hadn't been there all day. (*He pauses.*) I *still* can't believe it. It's like a nightmare . . .

DOCTOR. Yes. (*He pauses.*) I don't want you to take this in the wrong way—but you do realize that anything you say to me is in the strictest confidence? Even from your wife. It's impossible for me to help unless I know everything. If there's anything you don't want Mrs Preston to know . . .

MR PRESTON (*firmly*). I can assure you definitely on that, Doctor. I can tell you nothing more than I told my wife, and I told her everything I know. From the moment I left home yesterday morning until the moment I came in tonight I was absolutely convinced I had spent an ordinary day at the Bank.

DOCTOR (*sitting in the easy chair down* R.). Well—we must just try and explore and see what we can discover. Between the time you left home yesterday morning and the time you got back tonight, there's only one thing that *could* have happened. There must have been a lapse of memory that apparently lasted for a full twenty-four hours.

MR PRESTON. But surely when a man loses his memory, there *must* be a moment when he recovers it and wonders where he is and what's happened?

DOCTOR. No. Not necessarily. The return of the memory isn't always a sudden thing. It's quite possible that it gradually returned—that you gradually noticed familiar things around you and picked up the thread of your normal routine without even being aware of the lapse. I think that would be unusual— but it's not impossible.

MR PRESTON. But where could I have been for twenty-four hours? Surely *somebody* would notice a man wandering aimlessly about? If it was away in the country it might be possible: but it was London—and where could I have washed and shaved? Look—there's still a crease in my trousers—my coat and hat were perfectly clean and brushed.

DOCTOR. That's what we've got to try and find out. Have you been quite well recently—no headaches—or unaccountable restlessness—or sleeplessness?

MR PRESTON. No. I don't think so.

DOCTOR. Nothing seriously worrying you?

MR PRESTON (*after a slight pause*). Nothing to account for *this*.

DOCTOR. Was there anything unusual in your journey to London?

MR PRESTON. No. I got to the station a few minutes before the train came in. I met Major Watson on the platform—the President of our Social Club. We travelled up together and talked about Club affairs: the new tennis courts we're laying out, and the general meeting next month. I remember that perfectly. Nothing happened at the Bank because the Manager told my wife on the telephone I was there all day.

DOCTOR. Did anything unusual happen in your work that day? I mean any special problem or worry that might have disturbed you?

MR PRESTON. Perfectly normal day's work.

DOCTOR. And you left the Bank at your usual time?

MR PRESTON. Yes. (*He pauses. Hesitantly.*) You did say anything I tell you will be in confidence?

DOCTOR. Absolutely. I give you my word on that.

MR PRESTON (*rising and closing the door up* C.). Well, there's one thing. (*He moves to* L. *of the sofa.*) It's really such a trivial, harmless thing that it couldn't possibly have any connection with all this. (*He hesitates.*) You understand that my wife and I are perfectly happy together.

DOCTOR. I'm sure of that.

MR PRESTON. Apart from the small domestic arguments that everyone has, we've never had a serious difference in our lives, and we never shall.

DOCTOR. Mrs Preston told me that herself.

MR PRESTON. But everybody's got little things they like and dislike. My wife doesn't like alcoholic drinks. She's not intolerant: (*he moves down* R.C.) she's not a temperance fanatic or anything like that. I'm perfectly sure that if I wanted beer or sherry or anything else in the house she wouldn't raise the least objection. But I respect her feelings about this, and don't have them. In any case I drink very little and don't need them in the house at all. (*He pauses and perches himself on the downstage arm of the easy chair* C.) But like a lot of other men, I enjoy a glass of sherry in the evening when I've finished my day's work.

DOCTOR. So do I. Very much indeed.

MR PRESTON. It's been a habit of mine for some while to drop in at a little place and have a glass of sherry on the way to the station every evening.

DOCTOR. Well, why not?

MR PRESTON. It was just after the War. We were short of staff and I was working until seven every night. At six o'clock I used to go out and have my drink and go back to finish my work. It's a little pub in a side street near the Bank—run by a brother and two sisters—very nice people. The brother is around fifty, I suppose. Ellen is about the same age. The younger sister is much the younger—under thirty, I imagine. (*He glances at the* DOCTOR *with a forced smile.*) I know what you're thinking, Doctor.

DOCTOR (*hastily*). Not at all! Why *should* I?

MR PRESTON. It was all perfectly harmless. She's full of fun and I like her. We'd pass the time of day and have a joke or two while I sat there drinking my sherry. Then about two years ago this late work finished, and I was free to leave the office at the usual time at five o'clock. I was rather disappointed to think this pleasant half hour would have to end. They didn't open until six, of course—and I could scarcely hang about for an hour, waiting.

DOCTOR (*rising and standing with his back to the fire*). So you just went round to the side door? I used to do that at a place in Winchester during the War.

MR PRESTON. Yes. They live over the premises, and Joe, the brother, said I only had to go round to the private door and knock and go in, not as a customer, but as a guest. It was against the licensing rules—but it really wasn't a very serious offence. I suppose it was rather silly not to tell my wife, but I just let her think I still worked at the office until six and then walked straight to the station for the train home.

DOCTOR (*crossing to the stool*). Well—I don't think that's very terrible. I imagine a good many other city men do the same. Why didn't you tell your wife? (*He takes a note-book from his bag.*)

MR PRESTON. I really don't know why I haven't—mainly I think because I didn't want her to feel she was depriving me of something I could easily have at home. She would have insisted on getting the sherry in—but I didn't *want* it in. I like having it where I do at that time of the evening.

DOCTOR. Naturally.

MR PRESTON (*rising*). If I suddenly told her *now* that I've been doing this, she might think it was somehow connected with what's happened—but I'm sure it isn't.

DOCTOR. You went there as usual last night?

MR PRESTON. Oh, yes. I arrived just after five and left at six in good time to catch my train.

DOCTOR. Nothing unusual happened?

MR PRESTON. No. I just sat there in their sitting-room having my sherry and a sandwich. Joe was there writing out some orders. Then we all went into the saloon bar for a game of darts. (*He moves to the fire and stands with his back to it.*) I remember six o'clock striking from St Paul's as I said good night.

DOCTOR (*moving below the* L. *end of the sofa*). Well, then—it boils down to the next hour—because normally you would have been home at seven. (*He makes some notes in his note-book.*) Can you remember how you were feeling on the walk to the station? Or any incidents on the way?

MR PRESTON. I was just feeling happy and contented—like I always do, walking to the station after my sherry.

DOCTOR (*moving below the easy chair* C.). You mustn't think I'm trying to be rude—but did you have more than usual to drink that evening by any chance?

MR PRESTON. No. I'm certain of that. Two's the limit and they never press me. I'm very much a creature of habit, Doctor : one cup of tea for breakfast and then exactly one half more—and things like that. If by any chance I *had* drunk enough to put me out for twenty-four hours, I certainly wouldn't remember St Paul's striking six o'clock as I came out of the pub.

DOCTOR. No. I don't think you would. (*He pauses.*) And you arrived at Cannon Street in good time for your train ?

MR PRESTON. Yes. There is just one curious little thing. I don't think I'd even remember it if I weren't searching round for something out of the ordinary, but I do remember a curious feeling as I went into the station and looked up at the big clock. I can't exactly describe it : just a vague, uncertain kind of feeling. I remember looking very hard at the clock : so hard that I can see it quite distinctly now—the white face : the big black hands that pointed to a quarter past six.

DOCTOR. That may be something. (*He sits in the easy chair* C.)

MR PRESTON. Then I remember rather a dazed, uncertain feeling as I went for my train. I had to think before I could recollect the number of the platform—although it's always number five—every night.

DOCTOR. You remember the journey home ?

MR PRESTON (*uncertainly*). It's such a routine journey that I don't remember any special incidents. I think the compartment was full—and I think I had a nap.

DOCTOR. You slept on the journey ?

MR PRESTON. There's nothing unusual about that. I nearly always take a nap on the way home, and wake up by force of habit just before the train gets in to Bromley.

DOCTOR. Was there anybody you knew in the train coming down ?

MR PRESTON. I don't think so.

DOCTOR. You're not really quite certain about that journey ?

MR PRESTON (*after some thought*). Not absolutely.

(MRS PRESTON *enters up* C. *She is unable to contain her curiosity and anxiety any longer. She carries a tray with coffee.*)

MRS PRESTON (*standing in the doorway*). Oh, I was wondering whether you had finished ?

DOCTOR (*rising*). Yes, come in, Mrs Preston—do.

MRS PRESTON. I'm not disturbing you ?

DOCTOR. Not at all. That is, if Mr Preston doesn't mind. (*He glances at* MR PRESTON *for confirmation.*)

(MR PRESTON *rouses himself from his thoughts. He is troubled that his memory of the journey home is not as clear as he had hoped.*)

MR PRESTON. Yes. Come in, Janet, please.

(MRS PRESTON *moves to the coffee table and puts the tray on it. The* DOCTOR *closes the door up* C.)

MRS PRESTON. I've brought you some coffee, Doctor. (*She sits on the sofa at the* R. *end of it.*)

(*The* DOCTOR *wants to set them both at ease, and puts on a cheerful manner.*)

DOCTOR (*sitting* L. *of* MRS PRESTON *on the sofa*). That's very kind of you. Thank you.

MRS PRESTON (*pouring out a cup of coffee for the* DOCTOR). You'll excuse us, won't you? We're just going to have supper.

(MR PRESTON *sits in the easy chair down* R.)

DOCTOR. Of course. (*He pauses.*) Well, I think I can promise you one thing, Mrs Preston. Your husband's quite well in himself. I can see that without taking his temperature or feeling his pulse. A case of lost memory is disturbing, naturally, but there's no need to be alarmed. (*He pauses.*)

(MRS PRESTON *hands the* DOCTOR *his cup of coffee.*)

I haven't been your doctor long enough to know very much about you. (*To* MR PRESTON.) Have you ever had a serious illness or accident, Mr Preston?

MR PRESTON. No. Never. I've always kept very well.

DOCTOR. What were you doing during the War?

MR PRESTON. At the Bank as usual. I was an air-raid warden down here.

DOCTOR. You went through some bad bombing?

MRS PRESTON. Oh yes. We were right in Fly Bomb Alley here, you know.

DOCTOR (*to* MR PRESTON). Can you remember any specially bad experience?

MRS PRESTON (*to* MR PRESTON). There was that one in Elmtree Road, David.

MR PRESTON. Yes. I had a narrow squeak that night. A Fly Bomb came down on a piece of waste land just behind the houses. I wasn't more than a hundred yards away and naturally the blast was pretty bad. I wasn't hit by anything but I was deaf in this ear (*he points to his right ear*)—for a few days.

DOCTOR. Did you have medical attention?

MR PRESTON. I didn't think it necessary. I felt all right bar the deafness and that soon wore off.

DOCTOR. Well, shock of that kind plays funny tricks on you sometimes. We've had a lot of it since the War. Perfectly normal people may have a thing like this happen without even remembering the original cause of it. It may come from a severe shock, like this one of yours—or it may be the result of a long period of strain.

MR PRESTON (*anxiously*). You mean there's permanent injury?

DOCTOR. No. Not at all. It may be a good thing in a way. It may clear the system of a suppressed nervous condition. Once it's over, you are free of it for good.

MR PRESTON. If only I knew *when* it happened—and what I was doing for all those hours!

DOCTOR. I think we're fairly clear *when* it happened. (*To* MRS PRESTON.) Your husband remembers feeling a little queer at Cannon Street Station, Mrs Preston.

MRS PRESTON (*still half suspicious*). You didn't tell me that, David?

MR PRESTON. I only remembered it a few minutes ago.

DOCTOR (*to* MRS PRESTON). We've accounted for the whole of yesterday, until Mr Preston arrived at the station on his way home. We've got to find out whether his memory was actually *going* when he had this strange feeling he describes—or whether it was coming back. You see what I mean?

MRS PRESTON. You mean he lost his memory at Cannon Street last night, and stayed there until this evening?

DOCTOR. It's possible.

MRS PRESTON (*incredulously*). But surely the station-master or somebody would have done something?

DOCTOR. You could stay in a big place like that for hours without attracting any special attention. You wouldn't necessarily be strange in your manner until somebody actually questioned you. He may have gone into the restaurant and had supper; he may have gone out of the station and walked back to the City. (*To* MR PRESTON.) You haven't any dim recollection of anything like that?

MR PRESTON. None whatever.

DOCTOR. In the morning you may have gone to a barber's shop and had a shave. This evening you may have returned subconsciously to Cannon Street. The sight of the station clock, giving the usual hour of your return, may have been the thing that brought your memory back.

(MRS PRESTON *rises and stands* R. *of the coffee table.*)

MR PRESTON (*rising and crossing to* C.; *shaking his head*). I can't believe that. I know every inch of London—every street. If I walked about all night and all today, why shouldn't any one of a thousand other familiar things help my memory to come back until I saw that clock?

DOCTOR. Familiar things *would* tend to help, of course. (*He pauses.*) That's why I think it happened the other way.

MR PRESTON. What other way?

DOCTOR. Well—I'm not an expert in these matters, but I rather think that *losing* the memory is a more gradual process than regaining it. That feeling on the station: your confusion about the platform your train left from: the uncertainty about the people in the carriage—all that sounds to me like the period of *losing* the memory.

MR PRESTON. You mean it may have happened in the train coming home?

DOCTOR. You're not really clear about that journey, are you?

MR PRESTON (*uncertainly*). I've told you I *did* feel tired and drowsy in the train.

DOCTOR (*rising and standing below the* L. *end of the sofa*). Then I think that's what probably happened. Your memory began to go wrong at Cannon Street. You may have got out of the train at a station before Bromley. If your memory was failing—then strange surroundings like that would probably make the lapse complete. You'd just walk aimlessly away.

MR PRESTON (*irritably*). But where to—for all those hours? (*He moves to the easy chair* C.)

DOCTOR. That's something we don't know at present.

(MR PRESTON *sits in the easy chair* C.)

Perhaps in the morning—after a good night's sleep, you may remember some little thing that'll piece the rest together. (*He pauses. He is not very happy about his own solution, but he plays his part with a show of cheerfulness to help his worried patient.*) The main thing is you've got home—fit and well—with no harm done. (*He moves to* R. *of* MR PRESTON.) Naturally you feel disturbed and worried. (*He rests his left hand on* MR PRESTON'S *right shoulder*.) I'll send you round something to settle you down when you go to bed.

MR PRESTON. I never take things like that.

DOCTOR (*moving to* MRS PRESTON). It'll be quite harmless—if you can't sleep. And I'll look in about ten in the morning. (*He shakes hands with* MRS PRESTON.)

MRS PRESTON. Thank you, Doctor.

MR PRESTON. I must leave for the Bank at eight. I promised the Manager I'd be there early.

DOCTOR (*crossing to the stool*). I wouldn't go to the Bank tomorrow if I were you. Have a quiet day. Don't worry. Do the garden—go for a walk. As I say, I don't think for a moment there'll be any return of this. (*He smiles.*) Anyway, I imagine you carry your identity card. (*He picks up his bag.*)

MR PRESTON. As a matter of fact, I don't. It occurred to me just now. But I certainly will in future. (*He hesitates.*) There's one thing that's worrying me a bit, Doctor—about the Bank. It's practically certain I shall be Manager of the Eastbourne Branch next year. It's a good Branch and a good appointment, but it may affect things very much if the Directors hear about this. Naturally I don't expect you to make a false statement—but is there any way of preventing the Bank from knowing what happened?

(*The* DOCTOR *hesitates*.)

DOCTOR. Well—I understood from Mrs Preston that they *do* know. (*To* MRS PRESTON.) Didn't you tell the Manager on the phone?

MRS PRESTON (*moving in to* R. *of* MR PRESTON). Well—I had to. What else *could* I say?

MR PRESTON. You only said I hadn't come home? I mean, you never mentioned lost memory?

MRS PRESTON. Of course I didn't. I didn't know then.

MR PRESTON (*to the* DOCTOR). Supposing I said there was some misunderstanding? If I say I spent the night with friends and my wife had forgotten—or I had forgotten to tell her?

DOCTOR. That's entirely up to you. If I am asked for a certificate—then of course I would have to say what happened.

MR PRESTON. I wouldn't need a certificate for two days' absence. I could go back to the Bank the day after tomorrow?

DOCTOR. Oh yes. I think so.

(*A weight is lifted off* MR PRESTON'S *mind. He is suddenly brisk and happy and alert again.*)

MR PRESTON. I could say I was taken ill at my friends—stomach trouble or something—and by misunderstanding they didn't send the message to the Bank. (*He turns to the* DOCTOR, *anxious for his approval.*) You wouldn't say it was my *duty* to tell them what actually happened?

DOCTOR (*hesitantly*). It's no affair of mine what you decide to say, Mr Preston.

MR PRESTON. After all—you've told me I'm perfectly well and it probably won't ever happen again. But these Bank Directors are queer people. I'm sure they'd mark it down against me. (*He rises and crosses below the* DOCTOR *to* L. *of him.*) If I'd done anything wrong deliberately it would be different—but I haven't. Even down here it would affect me. If people knew—they'd always be watching me—thinking I was abnormal. Things would never be the same again because people don't forget. (*He pauses.*) You do see what I mean, Doctor? It's—it's not *criminal* to conceal a thing like that?

DOCTOR (*moving below the easy chair* C.). No. I don't see why. In any case, that's entirely your own affair. I'm only concerned if I'm asked for a certificate.

MR PRESTON (*happily*). Well—you won't be! I'll ring the Manager in the morning and explain. (*To* MRS PRESTON.) I know you'll support me in that, Janet?

Mrs Preston. I'll do whatever you think right, David.

Mr Preston (*shaking hands with the* Doctor). Can't tell you how grateful I am to you for the way you've helped me. Some doctors would have talked a lot of big words and frightened me out of my life!

Doctor. There's no need for that, I'm sure. Of course, if you'd *like* to see a specialist . . .

Mr Preston. Oh, good heavens, no! You've told me I'm in good health, and it's not likely to happen again. That's all the medicine I want!

(*There is a ring at the bell.* Mrs Preston's *nerves are on edge. She starts anxiously.*)

Mrs Preston (*crossing below the men, then to the door up* c.). I wonder if that's the Police Sergeant?

Mr Preston. You rang up to say I was home?

Mrs Preston. Yes. Just before I rang the doctor.

Mr Preston (*to the* Doctor). It's not a thing the police have got to *do* anything about, is it?

Doctor. Oh no. Now that you're home and quite well, there's no need. They may call in just to confirm things.

Mrs Preston (*at the door up* c.). He was a very nice man.

Doctor. If it was Sergeant Blake, he would be. (*To* Mr Preston.) I'd see him for a moment if I were you—just to show you *are* home.

Mr Preston (*crossing to the fireplace*). Then ask him in, Janet.

(Mrs Preston *exits up* c. *She leaves the door open and is seen to open the front door* L. *of the entrance hall.*)

Doctor (*moving to* L. *of the coffee table*). I'll send you those pills . . .

Mr Preston. Honestly, I shan't need them.

Doctor (*moving above the* L. *end of the sofa*). Well, go to bed early and have a good rest, and I'll come in about ten tomorrow morning.

(Mrs Preston *ushers in* Major Watson. *He is a thick-set man with a high complexion, bald head and bushy eyebrows. He is probably a temporary war-time officer who likes to use his army title. He is full of physical vigour and vitality; jovial, rather rough, and not very sensitive.*)

Mrs Preston (*standing* L. *of the doorway up* c.). It's Major Watson, David.

Mr Preston (*relieved that it is not the police*). Hullo, Major! Come along in! D'you know Major Watson, Doctor? President of our Social Club.

DOCTOR (*shaking hands with the* MAJOR). Yes. How are you, Major?

MAJOR (L. *of the* DOCTOR). I'm pretty good, thanks. I saw you at that Christmas dance of ours, didn't I?

DOCTOR. Yes. I came as a guest.

MAJOR. What did you think of the supper?

DOCTOR. Excellent.

MAJOR. Did you manage to get hold of one of those hot meat pies?

DOCTOR. Yes. It was very good.

MAJOR. You can tell a man by his friends and a club by its food. That's what I always say. (*To* MR PRESTON.) Have you roped him in as a member?

MR PRESTON (*laughing*). No, not yet. But I think he ought to be!

MAJOR. Of course he ought! Why not? Entrance fee a guinea: annual sub. two—that's all.

DOCTOR. Well—I think I could run to that.

MAJOR (*moving down* R.C.). Fine! You propose him, Preston —and I'll second him. It's the best Club for miles around: bridge, billiards—everything, including a monthly Brains Trust! —We've just been running a sweepstake on the Cesarewitch to raise funds for a new hard tennis court next summer—collected over five hundred pounds. Club takes twenty per cent so we didn't do too badly.

DOCTOR. Very well indeed!

MAJOR. I'd sell you a ticket if we hadn't closed on Sunday for the draw tomorrow.

(MR PRESTON *moves to* R. *of the* DOCTOR.)

DOCTOR. Well, if I'm a member next year I'll have a chance of winning it! (*He turns to go.*) Good night, Mr Preston. Good night, Major.

MAJOR. We'll have your name up for election at the Committee next Tuesday. There won't be any trouble with a chap like you.

DOCTOR (*laughing*). I'll try and behave myself! Good night, Mrs Preston.

(*He exits up* C. *followed by* MRS PRESTON. MR PRESTON *closes the door.*)

MAJOR (*nodding towards the door*). Nice chap.

MR PRESTON (*up* C.). Yes. He's quite a good fellow. (*He moves slowly behind the desk.*)

MAJOR (*moving above the easy chair* C. *to* L. *of it*). I was only thinking the other day we ought to rope in a few doctors. We've got a couple of chemists, but doctors give a club more class. *He pauses.*) What's he here for—aren't you well?

MR PRESTON (*behind the desk*). Nothing much. Just a bit of tummy trouble, that's all.

MAJOR (*moving above the* R. *end of the desk*). I wondered why you weren't on the train this morning. Been at home all day?

MR PRESTON (*playing the part he has decided upon*). No. As a matter of fact I spent last night with friends. Something I had for supper disagreed with me, so I stayed the night with them. I've only just got home.

(MRS PRESTON *enters up* C. *She is anxious for* MR PRESTON *to rest, and wants to get rid of* MAJOR WATSON. MR PRESTON *sits at the desk.*)

MRS PRESTON (*moving to the coffee table*). I'm afraid I can't ask you to supper, Major. (*She picks up the coffee tray.*)

MAJOR. That's all right. I'm not staying more than five minutes. I thought you'd have got supper over by now.

MRS PRESTON. We're a bit late this evening. I'm just going to cook some fish.

MAJOR (*jovially*). Well—when it's ready—just come in and throw me out!

MRS PRESTON. There's no need to hurry.

(*She exits up* C. *with the tray. The* MAJOR *closes the door. Alone with* MR PRESTON *he is not quite so jovial. He seems puzzled.*)

MAJOR (*moving to the stool*). You say you spent last night with friends? (*He rests his left knee on the stool.*)

MR PRESTON. Yes.

MAJOR. You mean you—you slept the night with them?

(MR PRESTON *hesitates. He is finding it more difficult than he expected, but having begun his alibi, he is going on with it.*)

MR PRESTON. I've just told you. Some old friends on the other side of London. I go there now and then.

(*The* MAJOR *stares. He is more puzzled, and grows anxious.*)

MAJOR. I came to see you about the sweepstake money. (*He pauses, enquiringly.*)

(MR PRESTON *looks at him blankly.*)

You took it away from the Club last night, didn't you? Robinson, the Club Steward, said you were there in the office at ten o'clock. You must have been pretty late for dinner with those friends of yours on the other side of London if you didn't leave the Club till after ten?

(MR PRESTON'S *bewilderment has turned to horror.*)

(*He looks at* MR PRESTON *in alarm.*) You *did* go to the Club last night and take the money, didn't you? (*He moves above the* R. *end of the desk.*)

MR PRESTON (*hoarsely*). I tell you I spent the night with friends.
MAJOR. You never went to the Club at all?
MR PRESTON (*defiantly*). No!
MAJOR (*breaking to* C.). Good God!
MR PRESTON. What did the Club Steward tell you?
MAJOR (*with his back to* MR PRESTON; *furiously*). Whatever he told me—it was a confounded lie and the man's a dirty low-down thief.
MR PRESTON. What did he tell you?
MAJOR (*turning slowly to face* MR PRESTON). He came round to my house last night to leave the keys because he was going off on his holidays today. He said he turned out all the lights and spent half an hour in his pantry clearing up, but just as he was going out he saw a light in the office. He thought he'd left it on by mistake so he went in to turn it out and found you there at the safe. He said it was open and he saw the sweepstake money—those bundles of notes—on a chair. He said you told him you weren't happy about leaving all that money in that small safe and were going to take care of it till the prizes were paid out. You mean that's all a lie?
MR PRESTON (*struggling to appear calm*). I've told you I wasn't there.
MAJOR. The damn thief had it all so smooth and pat I never doubted him. He was artful enough to say he quite agreed with you taking it because he thought himself it was too much to leave in that small safe. Then just when he was going he slipped in a bit that I understand now.
MR PRESTON. What was that?
MAJOR. He said you acted a bit queer and lost your temper and told him to get out and mind his own business. Knowing you never liked the fellow I didn't doubt that either. But you see why he said it? To make me wonder about you when we found the money gone—and give him more time to get clear. And now the dirty scoundrel's had a clear day's start.
MR PRESTON. Are you certain the money's gone?
MAJOR. Of course I'm certain! I went round this evening —five hundred and fifteen pounds of Club money—*Members'* money with the draw tomorrow night! We must get the police on to him at once. If they pick him up quickly there's a chance he won't have time to spend it. Can I use your phone?

(*He moves to the telephone, but* MR PRESTON *checks him.*)

MR PRESTON (*hardly able to speak*). Major Watson—don't do anything tonight!
MAJOR (*astonished*). Don't *do* anything! What d'you mean?
MR PRESTON. The—the scandal it would mean for the Club . . .

MAJOR (*above the* R. *end of the desk*). Scandal! Good God, man—it's a dirty barefaced robbery! He tries to throw it on you, and you say don't *do* anything.

MR PRESTON. There may be some mistake—some misunderstanding . . .

MAJOR. How *can* there be a mistake? The money's gone.

MR PRESTON. It may not have been stolen.

MAJOR. Well—if it wasn't—where is it? We counted the money ourselves on Sunday night and locked it up. If Robinson didn't take it, who did?

MR PRESTON. I don't know. I only know that I'm Club Treasurer and feel myself responsible. If there *is* a mistake, then it would be a terrible thing to put the police on to Robinson and accuse him if he is innocent.

(*The* MAJOR *stares at* MR PRESTON, *bewildered and suspicious*.)

MAJOR. Well—what's your idea? Sit back and talk and let the dirty skunk get away with it? You know we aren't insured against losing money.

MR PRESTON (*rising slowly; in a low voice*). I tell you—I feel responsible.

(*There is a pause. The* MAJOR *looks at* MR PRESTON *incredulously*.)

MAJOR. Well—it beats me. You never liked the man and you never trusted him, and when he does the dirty on us you want to cover him up.

MR PRESTON (*moving below the* L. *end of the desk with his hand to his head*). I'm tired tonight, Major. I've had a bad day— I'm not well . . .

MAJOR (*indignantly*). D'you suppose *I'm* well—after this? What are we going to tell the sub-committee tomorrow night when we meet to draw the horses? Pretend the money's still in the safe—then say we don't know who stole it—when we *do*?

MR PRESTON. Will you wait until the morning, Major? Let's decide then.

MAJOR. And give him another clear night for his getaway?

MR PRESTON. It's very serious to accuse a man until we're certain.

MAJOR. What are we going to know in the morning that we don't know now?

(MR PRESTON *does not answer. He is desperately tired. The* MAJOR *is more suspicious than angry now*.)

Well—I don't know what's happened to you. I thought you were a business man, and I thought you put the Club above everything.

MR PRESTON (*moving* L.C.). I'll ring you first thing in the morning.

MAJOR (*moving to the door up* C.). I'll probably ring you before you ring me. I'm President of the Club and I've got my own responsibilities.

(*He exits up* C., *leaves the door open, takes his hat from the hat-stand and exits by the front door* L. *of the entrance hall, slamming the door after him.* MR PRESTON *moves slowly to the fireplace and stands dejectedly by it.* MRS PRESTON *enters up* C. *from the kitchen.*)

MRS PRESTON (*closing the door up* C.). It's terrible, David isn't it?

MR PRESTON (*moving below the easy chair* C.; *sharply*). How did you know?

MRS PRESTON. Mrs Warren rang just now and told me. (*She eases above the easy chair* C.)

MR PRESTON. How did *she* know?

MRS PRESTON (*moving to* R. *of the easy chair* C.). It was in the late paper.

MR PRESTON. *What* was in the paper?

MRS PRESTON. Didn't Major Watson come to tell you? D'you mean he hadn't heard? They found Robinson, the Club Steward, this evening—in that little wood by the pond on the common. He's been murdered.

MR PRESTON *collapses slowly into the easy chair* C. *as—*

the CURTAIN *falls.*

ACT II

Scene 1

SCENE.—*The same. Nine o'clock the next morning.*

When the CURTAIN *rises it is a fine autumn morning and the sun is shining.* MR PRESTON *stands by the fireplace. He wears a dark lounge suit. He looks pale and tired. The door up* C. *is open and* MRS PRESTON *is in the entrance hall where she has just opened the front door to* INSPECTOR HEMINGWAY *who is in the porch. He is a big, pleasant, middle-aged man with a slow, deliberate voice.*

INSPECTOR. Good morning. (*He pauses.*) Mrs Preston?

MRS PRESTON. Yes. That's right.

INSPECTOR. I'm Inspector Hemingway. I called up just now and spoke to your husband.

MRS PRESTON (*in a dull tired voice*). Yes. That's right. Will you come in.

INSPECTOR (*moving in to the entrance hall*). Thanks. (*He puts his hat on the hat-rack and moves into the room.*)

(MRS PRESTON *closes the front door and exits to the kitchen, closing the door of the room before she goes.*)

(*He stands above the easy chair* C.) Morning, Mr Preston. I'm Inspector Hemingway. I spoke to you on the phone just now.

MR PRESTON. Yes. (*He pauses.*) Will you sit down.

INSPECTOR. Thanks. (*He turns, moves above the desk and looks towards the conservatory.*) Lovely show of those little dwarf chrysanthemums you've got out there.

MR PRESTON (*moving to* R. *of the* INSPECTOR). Yes. I—I go in for those.

INSPECTOR. Wonderful touch they give to an autumn garden. How d'you get such fine colours?

(MR PRESTON, *who feared the worst, is surprised at this friendly approach, and tries to respond in the same spirit.*)

MR PRESTON. Oh, I manage to get a little good manure from the riding school.

INSPECTOR (*easing behind the desk*). Not much of the good old stable stuff about these days.

MR PRESTON. No. I'm afraid there isn't.

INSPECTOR. Down my road the milkman still comes round with a horse and cart. The people all wait in their gardens with pails and shovels, hoping for a bit of luck.

MR PRESTON (*with a forced laugh*). Well—that's one way.

INSPECTOR. Trouble is horses are so regular in their habits that the same man gets it every morning.

(MR PRESTON *laughs again, and there is a pause. He is very strained.*)

Well, it's a bit of a shock—this Robinson business.

MR PRESTON. Yes.

INSPECTOR. I never met the chap myself. Stranger round here—wasn't he?

MR PRESTON. Yes. He came from the North, I think.

INSPECTOR. I got a bit about him from Major Watson this morning. Lived in rooms just off the Common. Lonely sort of chap by all accounts. Landlady says he's got a brother somewhere, but we haven't traced him yet. You're the Treasurer of the Club, aren't you?

MR PRESTON. Yes. That's right.

INSPECTOR. I suppose you know him pretty well?

MR PRESTON. Only as Club Steward. And he would bring the accounts and I checked them over and paid the money into the Bank.

INSPECTOR. Were they always in order—no trouble?

MR PRESTON. No. None at all. He wasn't a good book-keeper. There were small mistakes in additions—but nothing deliberate.

INSPECTOR. Did he do everything in the Club?

MR PRESTON. There's a woman who does the cooking, and a little fellow who works in the kitchen week-ends. He works at the hospital the rest of the week—so Robinson was practically on his own.

INSPECTOR. What's the name of the cook?

MR PRESTON. Mrs Pritchett.

INSPECTOR. And the name of the other chap?

MR PRESTON (*after a pause*). I don't remember.

INSPECTOR. I suppose I could contact him at the hospital?

MR PRESTON. Of course.

INSPECTOR. Major Watson told me a queer story this morning. (*He moves the chair from* L. *of the bay to* L. *of the downstage end of the desk, and sits.*) I think he saw you last night?

MR PRESTON. Yes. He came in. (*He moves the chair from* R. *of the bay to* R. *of the upstage end of the desk, and sits.*)

INSPECTOR. From his account this fellow had some idea of involving you, Mr Preston.

MR. PRESTON. Yes. Major Watson told me.

INSPECTOR. Of course, we've no proof yet that he took the money at all, because he hadn't got it on him when he was found, but if he did take it, he certainly worked out quite a smart little plan for his getaway. He was off on his holidays anyway, and

Major Watson says he told his story so convincingly that he might not have known it was a lie till the money was needed for the pay-out. I don't imagine he really thought he could involve a man like you. But that didn't matter. It was the time he wanted. Still, if he *did* think he could involve you he certainly wasn't in luck, because Major Watson says you were staying with friends on the other side of London that night. (*He takes a note-book and pencil from his pocket.*) Of course, we have to check up on everything in a case like this. If we don't then we're for it when we come to Court. They're always out to give the poor old police a dressing-down if they can. (*He opens his note-book.*) It's only a routine matter—but if you'll just give me the name and address of the people you stayed with on Monday night, we can clear that up right away.

(MR PRESTON *hesitates. He is fighting for his life now. He has decided what to say if the necessity came, and he tries to answer calmly and casually.*)

MR PRESTON. I spent that night with an old friend. His name is Wainwright.
INSPECTOR. Will you give me his address?
MR PRESTON. Seventeen, Manor Farm Road, Wembley.
INSPECTOR (*making a note in his book*). I was over there for a day for the Olympic Games in the summer of forty-eight. Did you see them?
MR PRESTON. No.
INSPECTOR. It was the day of the Marathon Race. I'll never forget that finish. Terrific! Pathetic in a way—that poor Belgian fellow losing in the last few yards after all those miles. You know—if you're sporting, that sort of thing nearly makes you cry.
MR PRESTON. Yes. It does.

(*The* INSPECTOR *closes his note-book, rises and replaces his chair.* MR PRESTON *also rises and replaces his chair.*)

INSPECTOR. Well—I won't keep you, Mr Preston. They'll need you at the inquest because this story Robinson told Major Watson will come in as evidence. But you'll know in good time. It's bad luck on your Club. Were you insured against that kind of robbery?
MR PRESTON. No. They won't insure money.
INSPECTOR. Well—let's hope we get it back for you. (*He turns to the window and looks out at the garden.*) I don't suppose you could spare a few of those chrysanthemums?

(*With an effort* MR PRESTON *manages to answer.*)

MR PRESTON. Of course. (*He moves to* L. *of the door up* C.)

INSPECTOR. My wife loves a bit of colour in the flat. We don't have a garden, worse luck.

MR PRESTON. I'll—I'll ask my wife to pick some.

INSPECTOR (*crossing to the door up* C.). You will? Thanks. I'll drop in and pick them up on my way home if I might, around five o'clock.

MR PRESTON (*opening the door up* C.). I'll see they're ready for you.

INSPECTOR. Fine. Well, good-bye. We'll keep you informed. (*He moves into the entrance hall.*)

MR PRESTON. I'll see you out.

INSPECTOR (*taking his hat from the rack*). That's all right. Don't you trouble.

(*But* MR PRESTON *moves into the entrance hall.*)

You're sure it's all right about those flowers? (*He opens the front door.*)

MR PRESTON. Perfectly.

INSPECTOR. I wouldn't like you to pick them if you'd rather not.

MR PRESTON. No. It does them good to pick them.

INSPECTOR. Fine. Well—I'll drop in around five. Good-bye.

MR PRESTON (*shaking hands*). Good-bye.

(*The* INSPECTOR *exits.* MR PRESTON *closes the front door, re-enters the room and carefully closes the door. He stands in thought for a few moments then moves to the telephone, lifts the receiver and dials a number. As he waits for the call,* MRS PRESTON *enters up* C.)

MRS PRESTON (*closing the door*). What did he say?

MR PRESTON. I'll tell you in a minute.

MRS PRESTON. Who're you ringing up?

MR PRESTON (*distracted*). Please, Janet—I can't talk if you're here.

MRS PRESTON. David!

MR PRESTON. I promised the Inspector some chrysanthemums. Would you go out and pick him some?

MRS PRESTON (*relieved*). Everything was all right, then?

MR PRESTON (*impatiently*). Yes—yes—it's all right.

(MRS PRESTON, *still puzzled and rather dazed, moves to the french windows and exits to the conservatory.* MR PRESTON *waits. After a few moments his call comes through.*)

(*Into the telephone.*) Is that Wembley seven-two-nine-four? . . . I want to speak to Mr Wainwright, please . . . What? . . . When did he go away? . . . Last Saturday . . . I must get in touch with him, it's very urgent . . . But you *must* know the hotel he's staying at . . . I see . . . No, there's no message. Good-bye. (*He replaces the receiver, moves to the stool and slowly sits.*)

    (MRS PRESTON *enters by the french windows.*)

MRS PRESTON. Did he say what colours he likes?
MR PRESTON (*vaguely*). Colours? What colours?
MRS PRESTON (*moving* L. *of the desk*). You said the Inspector wanted some chrysanthemums.

    (*The* DOCTOR *is seen approaching the front door.*)

MR PRESTON (*with a sigh*). It doesn't matter now.
MRS PRESTON. But, David dear—you told me a minute ago . . .
MR PRESTON (*helplessly*). A few of each—that'll be all right.

(MRS PRESTON, *worried, looks at him. The* DOCTOR, *in the porch, rings the front-door bell.*)

MRS PRESTON (*crossing to the door up* C.). I expect that's Doctor Sparling.

    (*She goes into the entrance hall and opens the front door.*)

DOCTOR (*cheerfully*). Good morning, Mrs Preston.
MRS PRESTON. Good morning, Doctor. Will you come in.
DOCTOR (*as he enters*). Well—how is your husband this morning? (*He puts his bag down in the entrance hall and hangs his hat on the coat-rack.*)

(MRS PRESTON *shakes her head, closes the front door and indicates the sitting-room. The* DOCTOR, *realizing that things are not well, nods and enters the room.* MRS PRESTON *follows the* DOCTOR *into the room, closes the door, then with a final anxious glance at* MR PRESTON, *crosses to the french windows and exits to the conservatory.* MR PRESTON *rises.*)

(*Coming above the easy chair* C. *Briskly and cheerfully.*) Good morning. Well—how are you feeling?
MR PRESTON (*with an effort*). All right, thanks.
DOCTOR. Did you have a good night? Did you sleep?
MR PRESTON (*wearily*). No. I didn't sleep.
DOCTOR. I didn't think you would. (*He moves to the fireplace.*) That's why I wanted to send you something.
MR PRESTON. You've heard what's happened?
DOCTOR. No?
MR PRESTON (*sharply*). It was in the paper.
DOCTOR (*turning and looking for a moment in the mirror*). You mean that Club Steward? Yes, it was quite close to where I live. I didn't know a thing about it till I saw the paper this morning. (*If any connection between his patient and the murder*

lurks in the DOCTOR's mind, he is careful to conceal it. *He speaks of it in a detached, impersonal way—then changes the conversation to his patient's illness.*) Well—have you been able to piece things together at all?

MR PRESTON (*hesitating*). No.

DOCTOR. No small thought or memory that might help us?

MR PRESTON (*shaking his head*). No. There's nothing.

DOCTOR. Shall we try running through things again—quietly and slowly, to see whether, perhaps . . . ?

MR PRESTON (*with a sudden nervous anger*). Oh, for God's sake, no! I did that in the night—for hours. I began to think I was going mad. I *had* to—but all the while I dreaded it. It was too horrible.

DOCTOR (*moving above the easy chair* C.). You mustn't think like that.

MR PRESTON. You don't suppose I can close my mind and not think at all? Why don't you say what's in your own mind and done with it?

DOCTOR. I know exactly what you're thinking. Every imaginative person who suffers a lapse of memory fills the blank period with all kinds of things that *might* have happened. If you hadn't read about this affair in the paper this morning you would have found something else—a burglary or something—and let your mind prey on that. You wouldn't be human if you didn't. But it's absurd to connect this matter of the Club Steward with yourself.

MR PRESTON (*crossing to the sofa*). Why is it absurd?

DOCTOR. Because a person suffering from lost memory still retains his own character, Mr Preston. If a criminal lunatic lost his memory he would probably continue to behave like a criminal lunatic; but a normal, honest man would continue to behave normally and honestly.

MR PRESTON (*sitting on the sofa*). Suppose a normal, honest man *hated* somebody—wouldn't he go on hating that person—subconsciously—when his memory had gone?

DOCTOR. If he *really* hated a person—then, yes—I imagine he would. But you didn't hate this man Robinson.

MR PRESTON. I *did* hate him.

(*The* DOCTOR *glances sharply at* MR PRESTON.)

How can I explain it? It wasn't the hatred of two men in the same station of life—who hated one another through business reasons or jealousy. He was just a Club Steward and I'm in a good position in the City. But from the day he came to the Club I disliked him. I opposed his appointment because of that, and I'm sure he found out that I opposed him.

DOCTOR. What made you do that?

MR PRESTON. How can I tell? I've never had bad feelings

for any man in my life except for him. Partly I think it was
because I enjoy the Club so much. I helped to found it and I
liked its pleasant, friendly atmosphere. Directly I set eyes on
this fellow I knew that he was wrong for a Club like ours. I
disliked his type—his big fat body, and his pale, flabby face.
Most of all I disliked his eyes—the way he looked at me. I don't
suppose I had any proper grounds for opposing his appointment.
He brought a good character from the Army—he had been in
some kind of catering job, and the Committee over-ruled me.
Naturally I was hurt at being over-ruled in a Club that I had
helped to found.

DOCTOR. Did he prove himself to be the wrong man?

MR PRESTON. He did his work well enough. He didn't drink
or anything like that. But the more I saw of him the more I
loathed him. I used to look forward to going to the Club, but
after he came I began to hate it. I felt his eyes on me every
time he came into the room. I felt something evil and horrible
about him. I knew he would glory in hurting me if he could,
and was waiting for the chance. (*He rises.*) Then gradually I
got a feeling that he was fated to ruin and destroy me. (*He
stands below the* L. *end of the sofa.*)

DOCTOR. That's why I told you to stay at home today and
rest. Imagination can play cruel tricks on a man.

MR PRESTON. You don't think I'm *suddenly* imagining all
this? For months now I've woken up in the night—fuming at
what this man had done to destroy my pleasure in the Club,
wondering what I can do to get rid of him!

DOCTOR (*crossing slowly to the fireplace*). But you've got to
be sensible. You never in your wildest moment thought of
murdering him.

MR PRESTON. Naturally I didn't.

DOCTOR (*moving and sitting on the sofa*). Then you're not very
likely to have murdered him on Monday night.

MR PRESTON (*moving to* R. *of the easy chair* C.). Do you know
what happened on Monday night? A few hours before he died?
He told Major Watson he saw me in the Club, taking that sweepstake money.

(*The* DOCTOR *is startled, but he keeps to his own course.*)

DOCTOR. Well—you can prove you didn't do that either.

MR PRESTON. How *can* I?

DOCTOR. By commonsense and reason. If a man were desperately in need of money—then he might be drawn subconsciously to a place where money could be found, but . . .

MR PRESTON (*breaking in sharply*). That *is* possible?

DOCTOR. If he definitely had theft in mind before his lapse
of memory—but if you're going to tell me you've been calmly
planning robbery and murder for the past few weeks—then I

don't believe you and I never shall. And what's more, I can't help you because you're making no attempt to help yourself.

(MR PRESTON *is silent. He moves above the easy chair* C., *then to* L. *of the desk.*)

MR PRESTON. You told me that sleep might help me to remember?

DOCTOR (*on his guard*). There's no certainty. A lapse of memory doesn't run to rule like an attack of lumbago or chicken-pox.

MR PRESTON (*moving restlessly behind the desk*). I hoped it would. When you left here last night I was hoping I'd wake up this morning with everything clear. But when I heard about the murder I didn't dare sleep. Reason told me that if my memory remained completely blank—then I could honestly defend myself against anything they accused me of. I could answer with a clear conscience that I had no knowledge or recollection. But if it *did* come back : if I *knew* what happened, then I'd have to tell the truth, or wait for it to be dragged out of me in Court. (*He moves above the* R. *end of the desk.*) That's right, isn't it?

DOCTOR (*rising and moving above the easy chair* C.). Depends whether your memory played the game or not.

MR PRESTON. I was dead tired when I went to bed, but I fought all I could to keep myself awake. I had a feeling that if I could get through just one night . . . I tried to call back old holidays at the seaside : I took myself for a walking tour in the Highlands and down the Thames camping when I was a boy . . . (*He sits at the desk.*)

DOCTOR (*moving to* L. *of the upstage end of the desk*). Then you went to sleep and dreamed every horrible thing on earth?

MR PRESTON (*shaking his head*). I didn't sleep. I never lost the sound of the rain trickling outside, and the trains and traffic in the distance. It began to come in little bits at first, like you said it would—queer little disconnected things—a chestnut tree —some strips of thin metal tinkling like bells—and a man's feet rustling through dead leaves. One side of my brain fought against it—the other side went probing on. Then suddenly it came together. I was on the Common, I saw every detail : the moon was shining and the wind was rattling those little metal strips the men hang round their allotments to scare the birds. I saw the pond where the children paddle and sail their boats and the line of chestnut trees with the dry leaves coming down and the two old dugouts under the mound. I was walking along the asphalt path beside the pond in a desperate kind of fear—and this man Robinson was following me—creeping along in the dark like a fat grey slug. I went between the trees and down the steps of one of those dugouts. There was a heap of old sandbags in one corner, and a square of that tarred roofing stuff. I laid the money under the square and emptied some sand over it, and all the time I could hear him up there—roaming about in the dead leaves. Then I went up the steps and looked out. I could just see him, going into the wood, and I followed him.

DOCTOR. When did you know he had been murdered?

MR PRESTON. Last night, when somebody called on my wife.

DOCTOR (*with relief*). Did this person tell your wife how it was committed?

MR PRESTON. I didn't ask her.

DOCTOR. How did it happen when it came back to you last night?

MR PRESTON. I followed him into the wood—then I—I tore my mind away from it. It was too horrible.

DOCTOR (*sitting on the stool and leaning over the desk to face* MR PRESTON). You see—perfect auto-suggestion. Doesn't *that* make you see reason? You dreamed what you were told by your wife——

MR PRESTON. I wish I could believe that.

DOCTOR. —you added to the dream what Major Watson told you about the stolen money—and you woke up when your information about the details came to an end!

MR PRESTON. What makes you so certain that I dreamt it?

(*The* DOCTOR *is not certain. He finds it rather difficult to answer.*)

DOCTOR. Because it's the kind of dream a man *would* have—after your experience.

MR PRESTON. You said my memory *might* return—so you can't be really certain?

DOCTOR (*hesitantly*). I can only weigh the two things together, and go for the one that's more probable.

MR PRESTON. If I were asked point-blank whether I remember anything of those lost hours—I mean if anybody in authority were to ask me on my oath—would it be honest to say that I still remember nothing?

DOCTOR. In your place I certainly would. If you were sure —then it might be different, but you're not. I'd give myself the benefit of the doubt because the law does that in any case. Whether it was honest I don't know—but that's what I'd do if I were questioned.

MR PRESTON (*rising*). I have been questioned.

DOCTOR. When?

MR PRESTON. Just now. An Inspector came to see me. He wanted to know where I was that night.

DOCTOR (*rising*). You didn't tell him all this?

MR PRESTON. No.

DOCTOR. Did you mention this loss of memory?

MR PRESTON (*facing the* DOCTOR *across the desk*). No. I

didn't do that. You see, I told Major Watson I spent the night with friends. He told the police, and they came to ask the name and address of the people I stayed with. I couldn't very well go back on what I told the Major, could I? I'm afraid I wasn't very honest. It all happened so quickly I didn't have time to think.

DOCTOR. What did you say?

MR PRESTON. If I'd gone back on what I told the Major and said I'd lost my memory—then I might as well have *asked* to be arrested. Everything in reason said I had the right to defend myself. If I could prove I was nowhere near the Club that night —then I was clear.

DOCTOR. What did you tell him?

MR PRESTON (*crossing below the easy chair* C. *to* R.C.). I told him I spent Monday night in Wembley with a man named Wainwright. He's my best and oldest friend. He'd do anything for me, as I would for him. I knew if I rang him up and asked him to tell the police—if they enquired—that I was with him that night—then he'd do it without question.

DOCTOR. Did he agree to that?

MR PRESTON. A caretaker answered the phone. Wainwright went off on a motor tour on Saturday morning. He stayed the week-end in the Lake District and he's somewhere in Scotland now. I might have known something like that would happen. (*He moves below the coffee table.*) Do you blame me?

DOCTOR (*sitting on the stool*). No, I don't blame you. I'd probably have done the same. But I'm afraid it's rather serious.

MR PRESTON. I'm sorry to drag you into a thing like this, Doctor. You're busy and you've got a lot of other people to see. What d'you think I ought to do? If I ring this Inspector and get him round—what shall I tell him?

DOCTOR. I wouldn't tell him anything if I were you—until you've had proper advice.

MR PRESTON. In what way?

DOCTOR. Well—I think a solicitor would know the proper thing to do.

MR PRESTON (*easing* C.). If I get a solicitor, the police will know at once I'm in trouble and trying to hide something.

DOCTOR. Well—I think you are in trouble. I don't think it's your own fault and there's nothing that can't be put straight —but if you try and do it yourself when you're tired and worried, you'll only make things worse. I know the first thing I'd do myself would be to get a good solicitor.

MR PRESTON. I haven't got a solicitor. Do you know anybody?

DOCTOR. Most people round here go to Mr Petherbridge.

MR PRESTON. I've never met him.

DOCTOR. They're an old firm that have been here for years.

It's all to the good to have somebody who knows the local police and the way to talk to them. (*He rises and moves to the door up* C.) I'll drive round and see if I can get him.

MR PRESTON. I hate the idea of a solicitor.

DOCTOR. It's silly to think that. I had one myself the other day. I got pulled up for speeding. You'll be surprised how quickly a good solicitor makes you feel better.

(MRS PRESTON *enters by the french windows. She carries a bunch of chrysanthemums.* MR PRESTON *turns and moves slowly to the fireplace.*)

(*Indicating the flowers.*) They're beautiful, aren't they?

MRS PRESTON (*moving below the desk*). Yes, lovely. The rain in the night did them good. The Police Inspector wanted some.

DOCTOR (*surprised*). The Inspector?

MRS PRESTON. He asked my husband. (*To* MR PRESTON.) Is he coming back for them?

MR PRESTON. Yes. This evening, I think. (*He turns and gazes moodily into the fire.*)

MRS PRESTON (*crossing to the door up* C. *and opening it*). Then I had better put them in water. (*She goes out into the entrance hall.*)

(*The* DOCTOR *follows* MRS PRESTON *into the entrance hall, leaving the door open.*)

(*To the* DOCTOR. *In a low, anxious voice.*) Is he all right today?

DOCTOR. Yes. He'll be all right. (*He picks up his bag and gets his hat.*)

MRS PRESTON. Ought he to have anything special to eat? I've got some lamb.

DOCTOR. Yes. That'll do quite well.

He opens the front door and exits. MRS PRESTON *looks in the door up* C. *at* MR PRESTON *as*

the CURTAIN *falls.*

SCENE 2

SCENE.—*The same. Half an hour later.*

When the CURTAIN *rises,* MR PRESTON *stands down* L. *of the desk. The door up* C. *is open.* MRS PRESTON *is in the entrance hall where she has just admitted the* DOCTOR *and the* SOLICITOR, MR PETHERBRIDGE. *The* SOLICITOR *is an elderly man, around seventy—with steel-rimmed spectacles and thin white hair. He is very stiff, formal and precise. He is no doubt a good solicitor and certainly a very careful one—but neither his appearance nor personality inspires much cheerfulness or optimism. He carries a brief-case. He hangs up his hat and enters up* C., *followed by the* DOCTOR. MRS PRESTON *closes the door, enters up* C. *and eases* L. *of the easy chair* C., *then down* C.

DOCTOR (*to* MR PRESTON; *as he enters*). This is Mr Petherbridge. (*He introduces.*) Mr Preston.
SOLICITOR (*moving down* L.C.). How do you do? (*He shakes hands with* MR PRESTON.)

(*The* DOCTOR *turns the easy chair* C. *to face* L.)

MR PRESTON. How do you do? (*He pauses.*) It was good of you to come so quickly.
SOLICITOR (*politely and formally*). Not at all. Luckily I was in my office.
MR PRESTON. Will you sit down?
SOLICITOR. Thank you. (*He moves the chair from* R. *of the bay to* R. *of the upstage end of the desk, sits, and puts his brief-case on the stool.*) Dr Sparling gave me a brief outline of the facts on our way, Mr Preston.

(MRS PRESTON *sits in the easy chair* C. *The* DOCTOR *stands* R. *of it.* MR PRESTON *moves the chair from* L. *of the bay to* L. *of the downstage end of the desk, and sits.*)

It's a thousand pities that you felt it necessary to mislead the police with an untrue statement. It makes it very difficult.
MR PRESTON. I was going to ring them up at once and explain. It was Dr Sparling who said I ought to have some help.
SOLICITOR. Yes. I think Dr Sparling behaved very wisely.
MR PRESTON. Now, of course, I rely entirely on you.
SOLICITOR. Yes. (*He pauses to think.*) I shall be obliged to ask you some questions that may seem unpleasant but a legal adviser must be in possession of the entire truth before he can decide upon the best means of defence. (*He pauses.*) If any detail is concealed—either deliberately or through carelessness or thoughtlessness—then his position is made very difficult indeed. Sometimes impossible.
MR PRESTON. If Dr Sparling told you everything I told him then you *have* the entire truth. (*He glances at the* DOCTOR.)
DOCTOR (*moving to the easy chair down* R.). Mr Petherbridge knows everything you told me—last night and this morning. (*He sits.*)
MRS PRESTON. My husband lost his memory, Mr Petherbridge.
SOLICITOR (*without conviction*). Yes, quite.
MRS PRESTON. You said something about "defence" as though he'd done something wrong. You surely don't have to "defend" yourself simply because you lose your memory?

SOLICITOR. I used the word "defence" in the anticipatory sense, Mrs Preston. Not as a foregone conclusion. You have to realize that your husband made a grave mis-statement to an official enquiry into his movements on Monday night. I'm afraid that in itself would constitute an offence in the eyes of the police.

DOCTOR. Mr Preston made that statement at a time of stress and anxiety. The police ought to be told that.

(*The* SOLICITOR *shrugs his shoulders as if he doubts it. He addresses himself to* MR PRESTON.)

SOLICITOR. I understand this statement involved another person—a close friend of yours who was in fact in no way connected with your movements on Monday night?

MR PRESTON. That's perfectly true.

SOLICITOR. That friend—by virtue of his close regard for you —might have felt compelled to support your request and declare that you were in fact in his house that evening?

MR PRESTON. He wouldn't have felt "compelled"—he would have done it freely and gladly—as I would for him.

SOLICITOR. You were asking him to commit perjury. If he had been at home—and if he had agreed, then he might easily have found himself committed as an "accessory after the fact" with all its unhappy consequences.

MR PRESTON. Are you for me or against me in this, Mr Petherbridge?

SOLICITOR. I warned you I would have to ask some unpleasant questions, Mr Preston. I should also have warned you that I would have to remind you of some unpleasant facts. In my experience a legal man is frequently handicapped—often to a fatal degree—by his client's under-estimation of the seriousness and dangers of his position. I believe it to be vital—no matter how unpleasant—to make things absolutely clear in a client's mind. It's the only way to avoid recriminations at a later stage —possibly the collapse of his defence at the vital moment.

MR PRESTON (*rising and moving behind the desk*). Then will you make one point quite clear to me. If a man committed a crime in a period of lost memory—would it be judged like a crime committed by a man in a normal condition?

SOLICITOR. That's extremely difficult to answer, Mr Preston. We should have to search for precedents and examine them. I've no knowledge of any *acquittal* from a crime upon the plea that the accused had lost his memory at the time when he committed it—although I've no doubt that the plea has often been made.

MR PRESTON (*sitting at the desk*). You don't believe that I *did* lose my memory?

SOLICITOR. I didn't say that, Mr Preston. If you tell me

upon your honour that you did in fact lose your memory, then I accept it without question. Our task will be to convince the police.

DOCTOR (*rising and moving to* R. *of the* SOLICITOR). Isn't it for the police to *prove* he didn't?

SOLICITOR. Certainly. That's the law. But I'm afraid Mr Preston has given them a tremendous advantage in making a false statement of his whereabouts on Monday night. A good Counsel might go a long way with that in Court. More especially if no convincing statement can be made to contradict it.

DOCTOR. I think there's another thing in Mr Preston's mind. (*He moves above the* SOLICITOR *to* L. *of the desk.*) I told you he had some impressions—personally I think it was a dream—last night. (*He stands behind* MR PRESTON'S *right shoulder.*)

SOLICITOR. You mean concerning this money?

DOCTOR. Yes. A man can imagine all kinds of things—but there *is* a chance of his memory coming back—in fragments—even completely.

SOLICITOR (*nodding*). You mean it may be difficult to decide what part is imaginary, and what part true.

DOCTOR. It's easy enough to settle about his dream last night—simply by going to those dugouts and seeing whether the money's there. (*He moves to* L. *of* MR PRESTON.)

SOLICITOR. I think that would be most unwise. The police would have men on duty in the neighbourhood of a murder. We should be inviting suspicion. In any case—even if the money's not there . . .

DOCTOR (*moving down* L. *of the desk*). It would settle Mr Preston's mind.

SOLICITOR. I know—but that's not the important issue. A dream which turns out to be imaginary is no proof of a man's innocence. Material witnesses and definite clues are the factors that really count.

MR PRESTON (*sharply*). What clues have they got?

SOLICITOR. I don't know. They may have none. Even if they have, they won't divulge them until the proper time. My point is this, Mr Preston. Even if your memory of those hours returns entirely—and we know that you had no connection with this crime at all—we must still produce material witnesses to prove it—people who can declare definitely that you were not at the place of the murder at the time in question. If, on the other hand, you were in fact concerned—then the police in their turn must produce the evidence.

(MRS PRESTON *rises and turns away to* R.)

DOCTOR (*moving the chair below the desk to its place* L. *of the bay*). I don't think for a moment he had anything to do with it—(*he sits* L. *of the bay*) but if his memory returned completely

—leaving no doubt in his mind that he *was* concerned—then how much should he tell the police?

(*During his next speech, the* SOLICITOR *opens his brief-case, takes out some paper and makes some notes.*)

SOLICITOR. In that case we must be guided entirely by Counsel engaged to defend him. (*To* MR PRESTON.) In the meantime, I strongly advise you to say nothing to the police but the bare fact that you lost your memory. (*He pauses.*) I'm concerned at the moment with the question of clues. Is there any personal property that you can't account for? Any small things that you had with you *before* you lost your memory—which are missing now?

MRS PRESTON (*turning*). Yes. (*To* MR PRESTON.) Your gloves and a handkerchief, David.

SOLICITOR (*sadly*). Oh.

MR PRESTON. I'm not certain about the handkerchief.

MRS PRESTON. You see, he usually carries two—one folded in his breast pocket, and one tucked in his sleeve.

MR PRESTON. The one in the breast pocket was there. I can't swear that I had the other at all—but I think I did.

SOLICITOR. Can you describe the gloves?

MR PRESTON. Brown leather. Almost new.

SOLICITOR. Had the handkerchief your name on it?

MR PRESTON. My initials—D.H.P.

SOLICITOR. Oh.

MRS PRESTON (*easing to* L. *of the sofa*). I embroider them on all my husband's handkerchiefs.

SOLICITOR. Of course.

DOCTOR. He slept in the train. He may have left them there.

SOLICITOR. Yes. We must hope that he did.

(*There is a short pause.*)

(*He rises and moves to* MR PRESTON.) Well, Mr Preston. At the moment there is only one thing to advise. Absolute frankness.

(MR PRESTON *rises.*)

I suggest that we communicate with the police at once and tell them you wish to correct your previous statement. You would then recount to them every detail you can remember of your movements between leaving home on Monday morning and your return on Tuesday night. Only that. Nothing at all about what you may have recollected—or imagined since.

MRS PRESTON (*moving below the easy chair* C.). What will they do then?

SOLICITOR. I don't know. It depends upon so many things—whether they have clues or witnesses to support them: the

extent to which they accept your husband's statement that he did actually lose his memory . . .
MRS PRESTON. But he *did*! We know that.
SOLICITOR (*moving to* L. *of the easy chair* C.). We have to prove it, Mrs Preston. Normally one does that by establishing an alibi. Unhappily your husband sought to prove a false one, and we've no means of telling what view the police will take of it. We shall endeavour to explain, of course—but they may feel their case strong enough to stand upon circumstantial evidence alone. They may proceed on those grounds. (*He turns to* MR PRESTON.) We must engage the best possible Counsel to defend you.
MR PRESTON. What will that cost?
SOLICITOR. In a difficult case like this you will need an outstanding man. If a person suspected of stealing can show himself to be in good circumstances—in no urgent need of money—then his position in the eyes of a jury is far stronger. That's why there is a psychological value in engaging an important man.
MRS PRESTON. I don't quite see what you mean?
SOLICITOR. I mean that an important Counsel commands a larger fee than a lesser man. If you can show yourself in a position to meet that fee, then automatically you show the jury that you were unlikely to have stolen out of urgent need.
MRS PRESTON (*crossing below the* SOLICITOR *to* R. *of the stool*). David! We . . .
MR PRESTON (*to the* SOLICITOR). What will it cost?
SOLICITOR. You mean the Counsel's fee or the whole defence?
MR PRESTON. The whole defence.
SOLICITOR. It's hard to say. (*He moves below the coffee table.*) I don't think it would be a long case. Counsel's fees may be—well—two hundred and fifty guineas.

(*The* INSPECTOR *is seen approaching the front door.*)

Expert medical evidence perhaps fifty guineas. If the case went against us, and an appeal were made—then perhaps another hundred guineas. (*He considers.*) I would say that five hundred guineas would provide for everything.

(*There is a pause as* MR PRESTON *sits slowly at the desk. The silence is broken as the* INSPECTOR *rings the front-door bell.* MRS PRESTON *crosses to the door up* C., *goes into the entrance hall and opens the front door. The others wait in silence, knowing who the caller will be. The* SOLICITOR *wanders to the fireplace, then turns and eases* R.C. *The* DOCTOR *rises, moves behind* MR PRESTON *and stands above the upstage end of the desk.*)

INSPECTOR (*in the porch*). I'm sorry to disturb you again, Mrs Preston. Is Mr Preston in? I'd like another word with him if I may.

MRS PRESTON. Will you come in.

(*The* INSPECTOR *enters and comes into the room. His manner has not changed. He is still quiet and friendly. He shows some slight surprise at seeing the* SOLICITOR *there.* MRS PRESTON *closes the front door, comes into the room, closes the door and stands* L. *of the sofa.*)

SOLICITOR. Good morning, Inspector.
INSPECTOR. Good morning, Mr Petherbridge.
SOLICITOR. Mr Preston has asked me to act for him.

(*The* INSPECTOR *nods.*)

You know Dr Sparling?
INSPECTOR. Good morning, Doctor.
DOCTOR. Good morning, Inspector. (*He pauses.*) I came to see Mr Preston professionally. I'll go if you like.
INSPECTOR (*moving to* R. *of the stool*). That's all right. Unless you've got other calls and want to go?
DOCTOR. I'll stay if you don't mind. (*He moves behind* MR PRESTON, *then down* L.)
INSPECTOR. That's quite all right. (*To* MR PRESTON.) I expect you know *why* I called again, Mr Preston?
MR PRESTON (*rising*). Yes.
INSPECTOR. Our Wembley station called at Mr Wainwright's house.
MR PRESTON. Yes. I know. Mr Wainwright left for his holidays on Saturday.
INSPECTOR. Yes.

(*There is a slight pause.*)

If you *knew* Mr Wainwright had gone away, I'm wondering why you told me you stayed with him?
MR PRESTON. I didn't know.
INSPECTOR. You mean you didn't know when you told me this morning?
MR PRESTON. That's correct.
SOLICITOR (*attempting to intervene*). If you'll excuse me, Inspector—wouldn't it be best if . . .
INSPECTOR. It's quite all right, Mr Petherbridge. (*He sits in the chair* R. *of the desk.*) This is just an informal talk, that's all. I don't intend to make any notes. (*He turns to* MR PRESTON.) The caretaker at Mr Wainwright's house told our people that somebody rang up for Mr Wainwright about half past nine. Was that you, Mr Preston?

(*The* SOLICITOR *sits in the easy chair* C.)

MR PRESTON. Yes. I intended to ask Mr Wainwright . . .

(MRS PRESTON *moves to the fireplace.*)

INSPECTOR (*breaking in*). That's all right. It occurred to me you may have given that information by mistake—that you stayed with Mr Wainwright some other time and got it mixed up with a visit to some other friends on Monday night. (*He pauses. He sees that* MR PRESTON *is under strain and tries to set him at his ease.*) When I called this morning I explained I only needed the information to rule out the story Robinson told Major Watson. I'm not asking for a minute by minute account of everything you did that evening, because a man can't often do a thing like that when he's suddenly asked. Monday afternoon I was off-duty and I went for a walk in the park. I stopped to watch a football match, but I couldn't tell anybody what time I stopped and how long I watched the football. You see what I mean? I only just want a rough idea.

(MRS PRESTON *moves to the sofa and sits.*)

MR PRESTON. I can't tell you anything of what I did on Monday night—or anything about Tuesday until I came home in the evening, because I had a lapse of memory.

INSPECTOR. I see. (*He accepts the statement without much surprise. It might almost be that he expected something like this.*)

DOCTOR. May I say a word?

INSPECTOR. Yes?

DOCTOR (*moving behind* MR PRESTON *to the upstage end of the desk*). Mrs Preston telephoned me at half past seven yesterday evening and told me what had happened. I came to see Mr Preston and I had a long talk with him, and I'm convinced that what he said was true. I'll be glad to make a statement if necessary. (*He crosses above the* INSPECTOR *to the easy chair down* R. *and sits.*)

(*The* INSPECTOR *nods politely and turns to* MR PRESTON.)

INSPECTOR. You would know about *when* you lost it—and when it came back?

MR PRESTON (*sitting at the desk*). I've been able to account for everything up to six-fifteen on Monday evening at Cannon Street Station. I remember feeling strange on the station. I had some difficulty in remembering the platform my train left from.

INSPECTOR. You mean you think you were losing it then?

MR PRESTON. I was either losing it—or it was coming back.

INSPECTOR. But if you remember everything up to the time you *got* to the station. . . ?

DOCTOR. We think he may have lost it on the station on Monday night, and it returned subconsciously on Tuesday.

INSPECTOR. You mean he spent the time round about **Cannon Street Station**?

DOCTOR. It's quite possible in that condition. He may have wandered through London. He may even have spent the night in a hotel.

(*The* INSPECTOR *nods. He does not appear to be very interested in the* DOCTOR'S *theories, and returns once more to* MR PRESTON.)

INSPECTOR. You don't have any little—shall we say—*gleams* of memory—any little memories that couldn't belong to other times?

MR PRESTON. No. I've tried to think. There are none at all.

INSPECTOR. Did you have everything with you when you got back? Nothing missing?

(MR PRESTON *hesitates: he glances at the* SOLICITOR, *who is sitting slightly behind the* INSPECTOR, *and the* SOLICITOR *shakes his head to keep* MR PRESTON *silent. The* INSPECTOR *turns in time to see what the* SOLICITOR *is doing. He notes it but makes no comment. Instead, he asks another question to save* MR PRESTON *from replying.*)

Nothing found—say—like a bus ticket—or anything like that? Anything that might show where you went or what you did?

MR PRESTON. No. I went through all my pockets in the hope of finding something. There was nothing.

(*The* INSPECTOR *nods. He does not seem very anxious to follow up the lost memory theme, although he makes no sign that he disbelieves it.*)

INSPECTOR. About this safe in the Club-house, Mr Preston. D'you happen to know how many keys there are to it?

MR PRESTON. There are three. Major Watson has one. I've got one, and there's another kept at the Bank down here.

INSPECTOR. I imagine you keep yours in a safe place?

MR PRESTON (*rising*). I keep it here with my other keys. (*He takes a bunch of keys from his pocket.*) My office keys: a latch key to the house—this is the key to the safe.

(*He offers them to the* INSPECTOR, *who does not want them.*)

INSPECTOR. That's all right. Robinson the steward didn't have one, then?

MR PRESTON. Oh no. There was no need for him to go to the safe. He had a till of his own.

INSPECTOR. You've got a key to the Club itself, I suppose?

MR PRESTON. Oh yes—with the others—here.

INSPECTOR. D'you drop in sometimes after the Steward closes up for the night?

Mr Preston. Occasionally. I've got a desk there, for Club papers. Sometimes I've walked round after dinner.

Inspector. You've no recollection at all of going there on Monday night?

Mr Preston. No.

(*There is a pause.*)

Inspector (*rising*). Well, now. I wonder if you'd just walk round to the station with me? You know it's one of our routines to take down a statement from anybody in any way concerned in an affair of this kind.

(Mrs Preston *rises and breaks down* R.C. *The* Doctor *rises and moves to* R. *of* Mrs Preston. Mr Preston *looks up with a start.*)

(*He tries to reassure* Mr Preston.) It's just a formality. I've taken one from Major Watson this morning and I shall be taking quite a few more.

(*The* Solicitor *rises.*)

Mr Preston. I'll do whatever you need.

Inspector. It won't take long.

Mr Preston. Shall I be coming back again?

(Mrs Preston *moves down* C.)

Inspector. Why, yes. Of course!

Mrs Preston. Would it be all right if I came too?

Inspector (*moving to* L. *of* Mrs Preston). You want to make a statement, Mrs Preston?

Mrs Preston. No. I think my husband would like me to come. (*She moves to* R. *of the stool.*) Wouldn't you, David? I mean, I'd like to wait for you.

(*The* Inspector *moves his chair to* R. *of the bay.*)

Mr Preston. I think I'd stay here, Janet—there's really no need.

(*The* Solicitor *moves to the* Doctor *at the fireplace.*)

Inspector (*moving to the door up* C.). I imagine you were wearing what you might call a " city suit " on Monday?

Mr Preston. Yes.

Inspector. D'you mind if we take that along? And the shoes you were wearing? It's just another bit of routine they make us do.

(Mrs Preston *sits on the stool.*)

Mr Preston (*moving to the door up* C.). If you need them, I'll get them.

INSPECTOR. I'll come along up and help pack them. Maybe you've got a bag we can put them in?

MR PRESTON. Yes, I've got a bag.

SOLICITOR (*moving to* R. *of the door up* C.). You've no objection to my being with my client when he makes his statement?

INSPECTOR. No. Not at all. We prefer you to. (*He smiles at* MRS PRESTON.) I'll try not to keep your husband's things too long, Mrs Preston. Good clothes aren't easy to get these days. (*He opens the door up* C.)

MRS PRESTON. I look after all his things myself.

INSPECTOR. You haven't cleaned or pressed the suit since he went to the City on Monday?

MRS PRESTON. No, I don't seem to have had time—we've been so worried.

INSPECTOR (*relieved*). That's all right. We'll be with you in a few minutes, Mr Petherbridge. I've got my car outside.

(*He exits up* C. *with* MR PRESTON *and follows him upstairs. The* SOLICITOR *closes the door.* MRS PRESTON *is nervous and finds it difficult to explain what she has to say.*)

MRS PRESTON. Mr Petherbridge—about those fees you mentioned just now. Supposing I were to pay them myself—could you do anything to prevent my husband from knowing?

SOLICITOR (*puzzled*). Well—how could we do that, Mrs Preston? (*He crosses to the chair* L.) Don't you think he would insist upon knowing who paid them? (*He sits.*)

MRS PRESTON. Could you perhaps say that the barrister had offered to defend him without fees—and let me pay the bill to you?

SOLICITOR. Would he believe that, do you think? He knows that professional services must be paid for.

MRS PRESTON. Mr Petherbridge, if I tell you something—will you promise not to breathe a word of it to my husband?

SOLICITOR. Certainly.

DOCTOR (*moving to the door up* C.; *tactfully*). I'll go.

MRS PRESTON. No—I want you to know, too, Doctor. I think it'll help you to understand why my husband seems so worried and difficult. You see, for a long time he's been terribly in need of money.

(*The* DOCTOR *and the* SOLICITOR *are startled and exchange a look. The* DOCTOR *eases* C.)

Oh, it's no fault of his own. It was his father—and it all began years ago, although I only knew about it last week. His father was an Agent of some kind. He travelled round collecting money for his firm. Then one day he couldn't pay. I believe it was betting. They were going to arrest him, but David saw them and said he would pay back every penny his father had taken.

He sold an insurance policy—but that wasn't nearly enough, so he borrowed some from friends and the rest he got from a moneylender. Well, gradually he paid back all his friends—he felt he ought to pay them first. But the moneylender kept adding expenses and things—and now it's—oh, nearly double what it was to begin with.

SOLICITOR. You say your husband only told you about this last week?

MRS PRESTON. No. He never told me. I saw a letter. I went to a drawer in his desk for something and I couldn't help seeing it. It was a horrible letter.

SOLICITOR. From this moneylender?

MRS PRESTON. Yes. It said if all the money wasn't paid in a month he'd tell my husband's bank and get them to stop the money from his salary. I *had* to speak to him about it. He was terribly angry. I'm telling you, Doctor, because I think the worry of it had something to do with him losing his memory.

(*The* DOCTOR *moves to* L. *of the sofa.*)

SOLICITOR. Why do you think he was so angry?

MRS PRESTON. He said it was *his* responsibility. But *I* was angry, too—because I've got a little money of my own—an annuity I bought with a legacy. It was a thousand pounds. Of course, it wouldn't be worth that now—but I could get something on it, couldn't I?

SOLICITOR. It could be arranged, I think. (*He rises.*)

MRS PRESTON. I wanted to sell it there and then, but he was furious. I think it was the first real quarrel we ever had. He said nothing would induce him to use my money.

SOLICITOR (*crossing to* C.). If the police happen to ask for any statement, Mrs Preston, I think you would be well advised to say nothing whatever about this.

MRS PRESTON. I wouldn't dream of telling them. My husband would never forgive me.

SOLICITOR. If you were asked about your husband's affairs, it would be correct for you to say that he never volunteered to discuss them with you.

MRS PRESTON (*rising*). Yes, it would. But you do see why we must pay those fees without my husband knowing? He couldn't hope to pay them himself—and he'd rather not be defended at all if he knew that it came from my annuity.

SOLICITOR. Yes. I understand that. You can be sure that personally I shall take no advantage of your difficulties, Mrs Preston.

MRS PRESTON. But I want to pay you, Mr Petherbridge.

SOLICITOR. My own charges will be purely nominal. But naturally we must face the fact that Counsel will require a fee.

MRS PRESTON. I'll never believe that David did this terrible thing.
SOLICITOR. They haven't said he did, Mrs Preston. It's possible they never will.
MRS PRESTON. They think it. I can see that. If they didn't, then why does the Inspector want to take away his clothes? They only do that to criminals—it's horrible.
SOLICITOR. It's something they always have to do.
MRS PRESTON. I'm sure he would like me to go with him. Do you think I could?
SOLICITOR. Of course. That's quite all right.
MRS PRESTON (*moving to the door up* C.). I'll go and get my things. I'll give you the annuity tomorrow. You *will* get the best possible man, won't you?
SOLICITOR. Yes. We'll get the very best.

(MRS PRESTON *exits up* C. *The* SOLICITOR *closes the door. The* MAJOR *is seen approaching the front door. He wears a felt hat and a bright red scarf.*)

It's very difficult.
DOCTOR. It certainly is.

(*There is an uneasy pause which is broken by the* MAJOR, *who rings the front-door bell. The* DOCTOR *crosses to* C. *and glances towards the porch.*)

It's Major Watson. I'll go and let him in.

(*He exits up* C., *leaves the door open and opens the front door. The* SOLICITOR *moves to the fireplace. The* MAJOR *enters and comes into the room. He places his hat and scarf on the* L. *arm of the sofa. The* DOCTOR *closes the front door, follows the* MAJOR *into the room and closes the door.*)

SOLICITOR. Good morning, Watson.
MAJOR. Good morning, Mr Petherbridge. Wanted to see Preston.
DOCTOR (*up* L.C.). You can't see him now.
MAJOR. Why? Is he bad?
DOCTOR. No. He's with the Police Inspector, upstairs.
MAJOR (*curious*). Oh? Why upstairs?
DOCTOR. I think you'll have to see him some other time.
MAJOR (*crossing quickly to the desk chair*). Well—it was about the Club account books. (*He sits at the desk and pulls open a drawer.*) I know where he keeps them.
DOCTOR. You'd better speak to Mr Petherbridge about that.
SOLICITOR. I don't think it would be wise to touch anything without police authority.
MAJOR (*closing the drawer*). Well—it's about our sweepstake. Preston's got a list of members and what they paid for tickets.

We've got a sub-committee meeting tonight. Lord knows what's going to happen.

SOLICITOR (*crossing to* R. *of the desk*). If you explain at the police station, I'm sure they'll do what they can.

(*The* SOLICITOR *hopes by this to get rid of the* MAJOR, *but the* MAJOR *shows no inclination to go.*)

MAJOR (*rising*). What's going on? Why can't I see him?

DOCTOR. He's not well.

MAJOR (*crossing to the fireplace*). I thought he looked funny last night. (*He turns.*) What's going on here? It's queer, isn't it?

DOCTOR. What exactly do you mean?

MAJOR. Well—all this. Last night Preston told me he stayed with friends on Monday—somewhere the other side of London—but I heard just now the police were looking for him.

DOCTOR. Who told you that?

MAJOR. Chap on the bus. Police rang up the hospital—wanting to know if Preston was there.

DOCTOR. You mustn't pay attention to anything Mr Preston may have said yesterday evening—because he was ill.

MAJOR (*moving* C.). He's always *been* all right. What's wrong with him?

SOLICITOR. He suffered a lapse of memory on Monday night.

(*The* DOCTOR *moves down* R. *of the easy chair* C.)

MAJOR. Good Lord! (*He pauses, and looks enquiringly from the* DOCTOR *to the* SOLICITOR.) That's a bit thin, isn't it?

SOLICITOR (*stiffly*). What do you mean by that?

MAJOR. Well—I mean it's a bit thin—that's all. (*He pauses.*) What's he told the police?

SOLICITOR. He's told them the truth.

MAJOR (*after an awed silence*). Poor old Preston. (*He perches himself on the downstage arm of the easy chair* C.) I'd never have thought it. And yet it always *does* seem to be that kind of fellow—I mean when you look at their photos in the paper—the kind you'd least expect. Have they got the money back?

SOLICITOR (*moving above the* L. *end of the desk*). I'm not aware that Mr Preston had anything whatever to do with the money —or the murder.

MAJOR. But you said he'd told the truth.

SOLICITOR (*deliberately*). That he lost his memory on Monday night.

(*The* MAJOR *stares at the* SOLICITOR *incredulously. He accepts this merely as a legal formality.*)

MAJOR. Oh. You mean they haven't got the money back yet?

SOLICITOR. I don't know. They've got that in hand.
MAJOR. Well—it can't be far away. (*He pauses.*) Aren't you *helping* the police?
SOLICITOR. Mr Preston has asked me to act for him.
MAJOR. Oh. (*He pauses.*) If he didn't have anything to do with it, then what's he want *you* for?
SOLICITOR (*moving to* L. *of the* MAJOR). For that very reason, Major Watson. It sometimes happens that an innocent man needs more protection than a guilty one.

(MRS PRESTON *enters up* C. *The* MAJOR *rises.*)

MRS PRESTON. Oh, Major Watson . . . (*To the* SOLICITOR.) The Inspector said would you mind coming up for a minute, Mr Petherbridge? My husband's given him permission to look round his room, and he'd like you to be there.
SOLICITOR. I'll come. (*He glances at the* MAJOR.) If you go to the police station and explain why you want to see the books, I've no doubt they'll help you.

(*The* MAJOR *nods, but has no intention of going.* MRS PRESTON *exits up* C. *and goes upstairs, followed by the* SOLICITOR, *who takes his brief-case with him. The* DOCTOR *moves to the door up* C. *and closes it, then moves to* L. *of the* MAJOR.)

MAJOR. D'you think they'll swallow this loss of memory idea?
DOCTOR (*taking a packet of cigarettes from his pocket*). Why not—if it's true? (*He offers a cigarette to the* MAJOR.) Cigarette?
MAJOR (*taking a cigarette*). Thanks. Don't mind if I do. Do *you* believe it? (*He lights the* DOCTOR'S *and his own cigarette.*)
DOCTOR. Certainly I do.
MAJOR. Why?
DOCTOR (*moving to the stool and sitting*). Because I talked to Mr Preston last night, and again this morning, and I'm certain he's not a man who would plan a careful robbery—then carry out a cold-blooded murder. (*He pauses.*) I've been a doctor for nearly twenty years. I've had a good deal of experience in judging people, and I'll stake my reputation on my opinion of Preston.
MAJOR (*beginning to see light*). You mean he really *did* lose his memory? (*He perches himself on the downstage arm of the easy chair* C.)
DOCTOR. I've told you so.
MAJOR (*sceptically*). But could a fellow do all this when his memory was gone?
DOCTOR. It's possible—but I don't believe he did.
MAJOR. What would they call it? Insane, or something like that?

(*The* DOCTOR *ignores this, but he feels the* MAJOR *worth questioning.*)

DOCTOR. You're an old friend of his, Watson?
MAJOR. I've known him ten years or more. I pulled him in when I started my Club.
DOCTOR. Then naturally you want to help him all you can?
MAJOR. I don't want to make it worse for him any more than you do. But I'm a soldier—at least I've been a soldier—and I've got my duty to the things I stand for. (*He rises, moves to* L. *of the sofa and picks up his hat and scarf.*) I'm President of the Club, and I've got to see that money back. (*He pauses.*) I mean, suppose he gets off—suppose they say he's innocent—that he didn't do it? Does that mean he can keep the money?
DOCTOR. Why are you so convinced that he *took* the money?
MAJOR (*replacing his hat and scarf on the sofa*). Well—it's bound to come out—so why not know it? (*He moves to* R. *of the* DOCTOR.) First of all, Preston was hard up. He borrowed money all round the Club. I lent him fifty pounds myself.
DOCTOR. But you were all paid.
MAJOR. Oh—he paid us back—in time. But I never knew a fellow get clean out of debt once he started borrowing. (*He moves behind the desk then down* L. *of it.*) You're a man of the world and *you* know that. Next thing—he hated the Club Steward, Robinson.
DOCTOR. Yes, I know that.
MAJOR. You do?
DOCTOR. D'you know why?
MAJOR. *I* don't know. Maybe Robinson had something on him over this money borrowing. Anyway, Preston was always bringing up fiddling little complaints and trying to get him sacked. And there's another thing. That safe of ours wasn't opened with a key. It was broken open.
DOCTOR. If Preston had his own key—why do that?
MAJOR. You don't have to be a Sherlock Holmes to work that one out. (*He moves the chair from* L. *of the bay to the downstage end of the desk and sits.*) He broke it open because he had a key, and Robinson hadn't. It was a smart job too. Nicely thought out. I never suspected anything because he hadn't touched the lock. He'd taken away the side panel.
DOCTOR. The side panel of a safe?
MAJOR. Well, it's more a strong-box than a safe. It just needed a screwdriver and a bit of patience. The police showed me how it was done and put back loose. I wasn't too happy myself about putting all that money in it, but Preston disagreed. He said it was okay. We counted the notes on Sunday night and put them away and locked them up. And Preston knew that Robinson was off on his holidays on Monday. See?
DOCTOR. I don't see anything but a few chance things that might happen any day to anybody.

MAJOR. You didn't see Preston's face when I told him Robinson had been round to my house. Men don't look like that about *chance* things.

DOCTOR. What did he say?

MAJOR. Nothing—at first. He looked awful. Then he pulled out that story about staying Monday night with friends on the other side of London.

DOCTOR. A man with a dark space in his memory can say anything on the spur of the moment.

MAJOR. When I said I was going to the police about the robbery, he pretty nearly went down on his knees to stop me. Would a man do that if he didn't *know* something?

DOCTOR. If he *was* at the safe, and Robinson caught him there—then why let Robinson come round and tell you about it before doing anything?

(*The* MAJOR *becomes more confidential.*)

MAJOR. He didn't *know* Robinson was coming round—that's why. I could see that when I told him. It was the shock of his life. I thought he was going to faint. Put yourself in his place and see what you'd do. You arrange to plant a robbery on somebody else—and the very man you're going to plant it on catches you red-handed. You tell him a yarn about taking care of the money yourself. He goes off. You don't know whether you've convinced him or not. Then you remember you've broken the damn safe open to make it look as if *he'd* done it. (*He pauses.*) All right so far?

DOCTOR. Perfectly.

MAJOR. Okay. You're in a hell of a jam. Besides—you want to keep the money now you've got it. You know Robinson's going home to get his bag and take the train to London. You know where he lives and you know the path he'll take to the station across the Common . . .

DOCTOR. How was the murder done?

MAJOR. Knocked on the head from behind—battered in.

(*There is a pause.*)

DOCTOR. Why are you saying all this against Preston?

MAJOR (*rising and replacing the chair* L. *of the bay*). I'm not saying a word against him. I'm giving you plain facts. (*He crosses to the fireplace.*) You want to help him—so why shut your eyes to what the police are bound to find out anyway? (*He stands facing the fireplace.*) I want Preston to have justice, but I want my Club to have justice, too. (*He turns and moves to* R. *of the easy chair* C.) I've given all I've got to that Club for ten years—and if we lose that money I don't know *what's* going to happen.

(*There is another pause.* The DOCTOR *looks at the* MAJOR *reflectively.*)

DOCTOR (*rising*). Yes. (*He picks up the ashtray from the desk and crosses to* R. *of the* MAJOR.) It looks bad for Preston —but then if you tie a lot of chance things together and throw in a bit of imagination it might look just as bad—even worse— for others—even for you.

MAJOR. For *me*! (*He laughs.*) That's rich. (*He perches himself on the downstage arm of the easy chair* C. *and faces the* DOCTOR.)

DOCTOR. Why not? Supposing *you* wanted money? Well —you knew where it was just as well as Preston did. What proof have you got that Robinson ever came round to your house that night at all? Was there a witness?

MAJOR. My wife was there.

DOCTOR. In the room?

MAJOR. She'd gone to bed. But she would have heard the bell.

DOCTOR. That's easy. You could have gone out and rung the bell yourself if necessary. You see—we've only got *your* word that Robinson came round and accused Mr Preston. Supposing *you* broke open the safe. As you say, it only needed a screwdriver and a bit of patience. Perhaps at first you meant it to look like an outside burglary—but Robinson catches you red-handed. Is there anything wrong with that so far?

MAJOR. Quite a bit. I was at the pictures all Monday evening. I got in a few minutes before Robinson called.

DOCTOR. Can you prove it? Did you go with anybody?

MAJOR (*throwing his cigarette end into the fire*). My wife doesn't like the pictures. I always go alone.

DOCTOR. You see? (*He stubs his cigarette end out in the ashtray.*) No proof you were at the pictures: no proof that Robinson ever called. (*He moves to the fireplace and empties the ashtray into it.*) You kill Robinson to keep him quiet—then you think of Mr Preston. You know it's common knowledge in the Club that he disliked Robinson, and you knew he'd borrowed money. Good. You also know he's a quiet man who spends most evenings at home. His wife might say he was in that evening but the police don't trust the word of a devoted wife. (*He crosses slowly below the* MAJOR *to* R. *of the desk.*) You go round to Preston's house to feel the way, and by the grace of the devil you discover this lapse of memory that makes even Preston doubt himself. It's wonderful! You're clear! Leave Preston alone, and his own imagination will do the rest.

MAJOR (*rising and moving above the easy chair* C.). You've got quite a bit of imagination yourself.

DOCTOR (*replacing the ashtray on the desk*). But you make

one big mistake. In your over-anxiety to settle the thing squarely on Preston you talk against him so much that you naturally make the police suspicious. They enquire into your movements and discover you can't prove a thing about that night.

MAJOR. I tell you I was at the pictures.

DOCTOR (*laughing*). When you tell them that old yarn they laugh. Every man trying to prove a false alibi says he was at the pictures. There was one last week. They're hanging him on Friday. (*He sits on the stool.*) As for Preston, he's in a far stronger position than you.

MAJOR. Why?

DOCTOR. Because his lapse of memory is too improbable to be a lie. If he'd said he'd gone to the pictures I would have doubted his word far more. But would any man in his senses commit a murder and then disappear for twenty-four hours without a single attempt to lay false clues—then walk back into his own sitting-room and try to make his wife believe it was the previous day? (*He shakes his head. With a smile.*) No, Major—that's absurd.

MAJOR. I never said he *was* in his senses. The shock of killing a fellow might make him lose his wits—then he wouldn't remember a thing.

DOCTOR. No. I don't think so. The shock might bring it back. It wouldn't make him lose it. (*He pauses.*) My dear Major, I know perfectly well you didn't have anything to do with it. I'm only saying how easy it would be for an innocent man to bring suspicion on himself by trying to incriminate another one.

MAJOR (*moving to* L. *of the sofa*). I never said I wanted to.

(*He picks up his hat and scarf, and puts the scarf around his neck.*)

DOCTOR. I know. I was just talking generally, that's all.

(*There is a pause. The* MAJOR *is not altogether happy. He is not quite sure what the* DOCTOR *is getting at.*)

MAJOR. Well—I'll get along down to the Police Station about those books.

(*The* DOCTOR *nods.*)

If there's anything I can do for Preston—just let me know. I'm not the sort of fellow to stand aside when a friend's in need, but I'm President of the Club and I want to see that money back. We can get a new Club Steward all right, because the labour situation's easier, but we can't get another five hundred pounds to pay those sweepstake prizes.

DOCTOR. I'm sure you'll get it back.

(*The* MAJOR *exits up* C., *leaves the door open and lets himself out of the front door, which he closes behind him. The* DOCTOR *rises, turns and gazes out into the sunlit garden. Then voices are heard on the stairs, and the* DOCTOR *turns.* MRS PRESTON *comes down the stairs followed by the* SOLICITOR, *then the* INSPECTOR, *who carries* MR PRESTON'S *suitcase, and finally,* MR PRESTON *himself, who wears a light coat.* MRS PRESTON, *who wears outdoor clothes, enters the room, moves to the fireplace and places the fire-screen in front of the fire. The others get their hats, etc., from the hat-rack.*)

INSPECTOR (*in the doorway up* C.). Well—we're going along now, Doctor. I wonder if you could drop in at the station some time this afternoon?

DOCTOR (*moving to the door up* C.). Yes. Any time. About three?

(*The* SOLICITOR *opens the front door and exits.*)

INSPECTOR. That'll be all right.

He exits by the front door and is followed by the DOCTOR, *then* MRS PRESTON *and* MR PRESTON *who drops the latch and slams the door behind him. They are seen going down the garden path as—*

the CURTAIN *falls.*

ACT III

SCENE.—*The same. Towards seven o'clock the following evening.*

When the CURTAIN *rises the window curtains have not been drawn, but the lights are on. The porch outer door is closed. Twilight comes as the scene proceeds. An electric kettle is steaming in the hearth.* MR PRESTON *is seated at the desk busy working at some papers.* MRS PRESTON *is* R. *of the coffee table. She picks up the teapot and fills it from the kettle.*

MRS PRESTON (*sitting on the sofa at the* R. *end of it*). Tea, David. (*She covers the teapot with the cosy.*)

MR PRESTON. Good.

MRS PRESTON. I thought you'd like some toast.

MR PRESTON. Yes. That's fine. (*He tidies his papers and looks across to* MRS PRESTON.) I've been sorting out a few things this afternoon, Janet. There's only the gas bill and the laundry and a small account from Rogers for the tulips. I've written cheques for those. You know the Bank pays my salary straight into Barclays, and that'll come in next Wednesday. (*He holds up a cheque book.*) It's a joint account, so you can write cheques on it yourself without any trouble or worry.

MRS PRESTON. I'm certain it won't be necessary.

MR PRESTON. I know, but I've always done these little things myself and I wouldn't like you to be confused and troubled if you were alone.

MRS PRESTON (*stirring the tea in the teapot*). I'm sure there isn't any need, David. If they were going to do anything, they would have done it yesterday—when they had you at the police station. But the Inspector was so nice when you came out of that room.

MR PRESTON (*switching off the desk-lamp*). Yes. He's a nice man. I'm lucky—because I don't think they're all like that.

MRS PRESTON (*pouring out two cups of tea*). He told me to see that you rested when you got home, and not to worry.

(MR PRESTON *rises and moves* C. *He has a sealed letter in his hand.*)

He wouldn't have been so cruel as to say a thing like that if he *meant* anything.

MR PRESTON. Yes, he let me go home all right, but he put a policeman to watch the house.

MRS PRESTON. You imagine things, David. There's *always* a policeman up there by the High Street.

MR PRESTON (*down* C. ; *with his back to the audience*). There was one there all night. I can see from my bedroom window. He was there at three o'clock this morning, standing under the lamp-post.

MRS PRESTON. There was one there when we came home from the Club dance last Christmas, and that was nearly three o'clock. I remember because we said good night to him. You're just tormenting yourself, David. Is it *likely* they'd let you go—and leave you alone all today if they thought you'd done it?

MR PRESTON (*moving down* L. *of the easy chair* C.; *patiently*). If you *were* by yourself, Janet—I wouldn't like you to live alone. I was thinking perhaps your sister would come—or whether you'd rather go to her?

(*He glances at her. She begins to cry quietly. Her back is towards him and he pretends not to see.*)

Your sister would have her pension, and you would have your annuity . . . Are you listening, Janet?

MRS PRESTON (*choking*). Yes.

MR PRESTON. It wouldn't be a great deal, but two women can always manage together. You might even start a kindergarten school again—like you had with her in the old days. There'd be room in this house. (*He pauses.*) Would you do that, Janet?

MRS PRESTON (*miserably*). I'd do whatever you say, David—until you come back.

MR PRESTON (*moving to the sofa and sitting* L. *of* MRS PRESTON). I had a talk with the solicitor this morning about that moneylender—and there's nothing whatever for you to worry about because he'd have no power to make any claim on you. In any case he probably can't claim anything at all. I've paid a lot more than he lent me and Mr Petherbridge says a solicitor's letter will settle it. I'm telling you because—if he *did* write to you, then give the letter straight to Mr Petherbridge. Don't answer it, and above all don't dream of doing anything silly—like raising money on that little annuity of yours and sending it to him. You promise me that?

MRS PRESTON. Yes.

MR PRESTON. I've written to the Bank. (*He shows her the letter and puts it on the table.*) I want you to post this if they take me away. I've explained everything and I'm sure they'll do something for you after all the years I've been there.

MRS PRESTON. You mustn't talk like this, David. I can't bear it!

MR PRESTON. I know, Janet—but you see, *I* couldn't bear it if I had to go away without feeling we had arranged everything we possibly could. It's so simple now, sitting here by ourselves. Afterwards I don't think they'd let us be alone together. (*He rises and moves restlessly to* L.C.)

MRS PRESTON (*rising*). Even if they *did* take you away—they couldn't treat you like a criminal. (*She refills the teapot from the kettle.*) Dr Sparling says they can't possibly do that. It wouldn't be human to blame you for something that happened when you weren't yourself.

MR PRESTON (*moving to* L. *of the sofa*). We have to face these things, dear. Even if they believe me when I say I wasn't myself that night—they still wouldn't let me go. They couldn't. They've got a place for people who do things when they're not themselves. (*He pauses.*) And then we're not certain they'll believe I lost my memory at all.

MRS PRESTON (*resuming her seat on the sofa*). But it's true, David! It *is* true, isn't it?

MR PRESTON. I swear that, Janet. Whatever happened that night, I knew nothing about it. I did nothing deliberately.

MRS PRESTON. Those things you *thought* you remembered. You mustn't tell them that.

MR PRESTON. If they ask me in the Court, then I'm afraid I would have to.

MRS PRESTON. But Mr Petherbridge said " no ".

MR PRESTON. He told me not to in my statement to the police, that's all. You see, these men who cross-examine you can tell at once when you're lying or holding anything back. They've got a way of tearing things out of you, and they go on and on until they do. I couldn't bear the indignity of having that done to me. At least I can keep my self-respect, Janet. (*He sits on the sofa,* L. *of* MRS PRESTON.) If I can do that—then I don't mind what happens, so long as you promise to carry on and be happy.

MRS PRESTON. How *could* I be happy?

MR PRESTON. By believing in me, dear. By trusting me when I tell you I didn't do this deliberately. It'll mean so much to me if you do that. You've always got on well with your sister. Start that little school again. It'll give you something interesting and help you along. In any case you'll always have that little annuity. Nobody can take that away, so you'll never have to be dependent on anybody.

MRS PRESTON. I still think it won't happen, David. It's just your imagination all the time. Last night and all this morning I was listening, thinking they might come—but now, why, it's more than a full day and I'm certain it's all right. Look—I took a lot of trouble with this toast and it's real butter.

MR PRESTON (*taking a piece of toast*). You always knew the way to make toast. (*He tries to eat it, and drink his tea.*)

MRS PRESTON. You haven't slept or even rested properly since you came home. Lie down after tea and try to get some sleep.

MR PRESTON (*rising with his cup and saucer in his hand*). Yes. I think that's a good idea. (*He moves to the fireplace.*)

MRS PRESTON. At seven o'clock we'll have supper—then why not go to the pictures? It's our night, isn't it?
MR PRESTON. Yes. I forgot that. Thursday. (*He puts his cup and saucer on the mantelpiece.*)
MRS PRESTON (*rising and moving below the coffee table to* MR PRESTON). They didn't say you'd got to stay in. We'll say " good evening " to that policeman at the corner and you'll see he'll say " good evening " back, and not take a bit of notice—and you'll wonder why you've been so silly.
MR PRESTON (*with a laugh*). Can't think why you're so good to me. (*He takes her by the shoulders and kisses her.*)
MRS PRESTON (*breaking to* L. *of the sofa*). It's you that are always good to me. (*She pauses and turns.*) You *will* go and try and rest, won't you?
MR PRESTON (*smiling reassuringly*). Yes. (*He crosses to the desk.*) Now don't you worry. You just go ahead and get supper. (*He picks up a small account book from the desk and moves to* L. *of* MRS PRESTON.) I'd like you to have a glance through this account book and see that you understand it. Let me know if there's anything you don't. (*He opens the book and indicates the entries.*) It's quite simple, really—what I receive here—and payments there. There isn't much at the moment but there'll be nearly one hundred pounds when my salary comes in next Wednesday. (*He closes the book and hands it to her.*)
MRS PRESTON. And now you don't owe anything?
MR PRESTON. Nothing.
MRS PRESTON. We'll save up and go abroad again next summer.
MR PRESTON. Yes. We'll do that.
MRS PRESTON. Draw the curtains and have a good sleep.
MR PRESTON (*opening the door up* C.). I've a few things to tidy up, and then I will.
MRS PRESTON. I'll come up and call you when supper's ready —then the cinema.
MR PRESTON (*moving to the stairs*). That'll be fine.

(*With a foot on the bottom step he pauses, turns, gives her a smile, then exits up the stairs.* MRS PRESTON *keeps her own cheerfulness until he has gone, then her brave attempt at make-believe falls away. She moves behind the desk and puts the account book in the desk drawer. As she does so, she sees the* MAJOR *approaching the front door. She moves quickly to the entrance hall, switches on the porch light and opens the porch outer door before the* MAJOR *has time to ring the bell.*)

MAJOR. Good evening, Mrs Preston. Can I come in?

(*He enters and comes into the room.* MRS PRESTON *closes the doors and follows him in.*)

Is your husband at home?

Mrs Preston (*closing the door up* C.). He's at home, Major, but he's very tired and trying to rest. Is there anything I can do?

Major (*moving to the fireplace*). Well, I was just wondering if anything had happened since he went round to the police station yesterday?

Mrs Preston (*moving* C.). Nothing.

Major. Funny. I wonder what they're doing? Have they said anything?

Mrs Preston. No. I'm sorry, Major, there's nothing I can tell you.

Major. Well, there's something I can tell *you*, Mrs Preston. I've got some good news for you.

Mrs Preston. You have?

Major. Yes. You know your husband's one of my oldest friends. I couldn't sleep last night—thinking about him with no-one to help him—and suddenly I realized that somebody's got to take the lead—*publicly*—and organize his defence.

Mrs Preston. But you said you had some good news.

Major. That's what I'm telling you. (*He moves to* R. *of* Mrs Preston.) It's got to be somebody whose name goes for something around here, so I've called a Special Meeting of the Club Committee for nine o'clock this evening, and I'm going to put it to them in the form of a resolution: " That this Committee hereby declares its determination to stand by a fellow member in misfortune——"

Mrs Preston. But, Major . . .

Major. Wait a minute—that's not all—" to stand by a fellow member in misfortune, and open a fund for his defence." And to show I'm not just a man of words I'm going to put up a fiver myself to start things off.

Mrs Preston. But they haven't accused him, Major—and I don't believe they will, now. I'm certain they don't think he did it.

Major. What makes you think that?

Mrs Preston (*moving up* L.C.). Something the Inspector said.

Major. Why? Have they got another idea—what did he say?

Mrs Preston. He told me not to worry.

Major (*moving to* R. *of* Mrs Preston). Oh, well, I don't think that means anything. They always say that kind of thing—besides, if they didn't think he did it, why put a policeman up there at the corner?

Mrs Preston. You think he did it! There's something you're not telling me, Major.

Major (*turning and moving to the fireplace*). Me? There's nothing *I'm* not telling you. Maybe *he* hasn't told you everything.

Mrs Preston (*moving to* R. *of the easy chair* C.). Why do you say that? There is something you know. What is it?

Major (*hesitatingly*). Well—it's the chap who lives next door to our Club. Just about ten on Monday night he was down his garden when he saw two men come out of the back door of the Club and walk across the yard. He's pretty certain one of them was your husband, and he thinks the other was Robinson because he recognized his north country accent. He couldn't hear much of what they said, but he's certain of one thing—they weren't quarrelling. In fact, they sounded pretty thick together and making some sort of plans.

Mrs Preston (*sitting in the easy chair* C.). That's impossible, Major. My husband never liked Robinson—he wouldn't even talk to him if he could help it.

Major. Maybe he *had* to talk to him. Maybe Robinson caught him at the safe and put on a little blackmail—fifty-fifty to keep his mouth shut, or something like that. They went out the back gate together and down the lane. They stood talking at the corner—then one went one way and the other went the other.

Mrs Preston. It couldn't have been my husband.

Major. Well—who could it have been? It wasn't *me*! I was at the pictures. (*He moves to* R. *of* Mrs Preston.) I was only thinking you might want to tell that lawyer of yours, because it doesn't seem to make sense of that lost memory idea.

Mrs Preston. Has this man told the police?

Major (*nodding*). Last night. That's what made me wonder why you hadn't heard anything.

(*There is a pause. Then the* Major *catches sight of* Peggy Dobson *through the window as she approaches the front door.*)

There's someone coming in your gate.

(Mrs Preston *rises and goes quickly out into the porch and opens the outer door before* Peggy *has time to ring the bell. She leaves the room and front doors open.* Peggy *is very attractive in a plump, fair-haired, buxom way. She looks like a good-class barmaid—smartly but not over-dressed. She has a slight cockney accent but makes no pretensions. She is natural and likeable.*)

Peggy. Oh—good evening—does Mr Preston live here?

(*The* Major *moves to* R. *of the door up* C. *to overhear the conversation.*)

Mrs Preston. Yes.
Peggy. Are you Mrs Preston?
Mrs Preston. Yes.
Peggy. Could I see Mr Preston, please?
Mrs Preston. He's resting and I can't disturb him now.

Act III]   HOME AT SEVEN   61

PEGGY. Well—it's about this trouble—this murder.
MRS PRESTON. You'd better come in.

(PEGGY *enters and comes into the room.* MRS PRESTON *follows her in, leaving the doors open.*)

MAJOR (*to* PEGGY, *as she enters*). Good evening—are you from the papers?
PEGGY. No, I'm not. I'm a friend of Mr Preston's.
MAJOR. That's what I am.
MRS PRESTON (*the open door in her hand; waiting to get rid of the* MAJOR). I'll tell my husband what you said about the committee, Major. I'm sure he'll be grateful.
MAJOR (*moving into the entrance hall*). Well, the great thing is to let people know there's public opinion on his side and somebody's leading it. Let him know I'm standing by—and give me a ring when you want me.
MRS PRESTON. Thank you, Major.

(*With a final look at* PEGGY, *the* MAJOR *exits.* MRS PRESTON *closes the front door then enters the room and closes the door deliberately behind her.*)

PEGGY (L. *of the sofa; with a laugh*). You see, I'm really quite an old friend of Mr Preston's, and I thought I might be able to help him.

(MRS PRESTON *looks sharply at* PEGGY, *with growing suspicion and dislike.*)

MRS PRESTON (*crossing to the fireplace*). I think I know most of my husband's friends.
PEGGY. Well, I expect you do—but I don't suppose Dave ever told you about me.
MRS PRESTON (*angry and incredulous*). Dave?
PEGGY (*correcting herself with a nervous laugh*). Well—Mr Preston. He always let me call him Dave, but I'm sorry. (*She pauses.*) Is he in trouble about this murder—I mean, *really* in trouble? (*She pauses.*)

(MRS PRESTON *hesitates. She cannot make up her mind what to do.*)

Because if he is, I want to help him, and I think I can.
MRS PRESTON (*still doubtful*). Then won't you sit down.

(PEGGY *sits on the sofa at the* L. *end of it.* MRS PRESTON *switches on the table-lamp down* R.)

PEGGY (*looking around*). You live in a nice house.
MRS PRESTON. Yes. (*She pauses.*) You haven't told me your name.
PEGGY. Miss Dobson. Peggy Dobson. I work with my brother and sister at *The Feathers* in River Lane—just off Queen Victoria Street—in the City, you know.

E

MRS PRESTON. *The Feathers?*
PEGGY. It's a public house. Our own place.
MRS PRESTON (*after a pause*). What is it that you want to say? (*She moves the cup and saucer from the mantelpiece on to the tray.*)
PEGGY. Well—I came straight down as quickly as I could because I only heard about this trouble at lunch-time.
MRS PRESTON. Mr Preston's name hasn't been in the papers. How did you know he was in trouble? (*She picks up the letter from the coffee table and puts it on the mantelpiece.*)
PEGGY. Well—a young man who has lunch at our place comes from down here, and he told us how they took Mr Preston round to the police station yesterday. Of course we'd read about this awful murder in the papers, but even if they *had* mentioned him we might never have known it was *our* Mr Preston.
MRS PRESTON. *Your* Mr Preston?
PEGGY. I know. It's funny. We've known him all these years and we never knew where he came from! We only realized when this young man said—" You know that fellow Preston who comes here in the evening?—they're after him for that Bromley murder "—and of course I saw at once I'd got to come. He told me the road but I had to ask a policeman up there at the corner which house it was. He gave me such a queer look I knew things must be bad.
MRS PRESTON (*crossing to* L.C.). Yes, they are bad. Why did you come? What is it about?
PEGGY. Well, everything. Last Monday night. You see, Mr Preston's been coming to our place—oh, ever since the War. He just drops in of an evening—on his way home. (*She sees the increasing suspicion and hostility in* MRS PRESTON'S *face and begins to get angry. She rises.*) Look—if you think there's anything in it, you're wrong—because there isn't. I'm not the sort that runs after other people's husbands and I never did.
MRS PRESTON (*coldly*). I didn't suggest it, Miss Dobson.
PEGGY. No, but you're *looking* it, anybody can see that. It's no good talking if you aren't going to listen. Why don't you bring him down and let me tell *him*?

(MRS PRESTON *has no intention of bringing her husband down. She is determined to find out for herself what her visitor has come for.*)

MRS PRESTON. I've told you. My husband's very tired and trying to rest. If you've anything to say, you can tell *me*.
PEGGY (*still injured*). *The Feathers* is respectable. You can ask anybody. All he ever had was a sherry and a sandwich, maybe. Sometimes we'd just sit round chatting in our private room . . .

MRS PRESTON. Your *private* room?

PEGGY. Because he came before we opened, that's why. Sometimes we'd go into the saloon bar and have a game of darts —but he always left on the stroke of six to catch his train at Cannon Street.

MRS PRESTON (*moving to* L. *of* PEGGY). You say he's done this for a long time? (*She sits in the easy chair* C.)

PEGGY. Oh, every evening regular—getting on for five years now. I'm sure it does him good because he looks so tired and worried sometimes when he comes in, but he always goes away feeling better. (*She pauses.*) Don't *you* think he's been looking bad lately?

MRS PRESTON. Won't you sit down again. Yes, he's been rather worried recently.

PEGGY (*sitting on the sofa*). Well—we thought he looked specially tired on Monday night, so I gave him a Bovril sandwich with his glass of sherry. Then we went into the saloon bar for a game of darts. It was empty at that time of course, because we weren't open—but we always draw the blinds to be on the safe side. Anyway, Mr Preston's quite good at darts, you know. I was playing with him against my brother and sister and we were leading. We were laughing and joking, and then the strangest thing happened. There's a little van that brings our sandwiches from a place in Hornsey. It's more convenient to get our sandwiches like that. It comes about half-past five and George, the barman, takes the stuff in. Well, it finished unloading, and just as it was starting off it had a terrific backfire —you know—like a gun going off. We all jumped because it startled us—and Mr Preston did, too. He turned his head quickly—and when he turned it back—he looked different.

MRS PRESTON. How do you mean—he looked *different*?

PEGGY. Well—you know when you turn your head quickly and rick your neck? It was just as if Mr Preston ricked his brain. It sounds funny, but that's exactly what happened and exactly what it looked like. I can't explain because of course I'm not a doctor or anything like that. His face just went different. He looked round as if he didn't know where he was, and dropped the dart he had in his hand and sat down. Of course it scared us because we thought he was suddenly taken ill—but he kept saying he was *quite* all right in a queer sort of way. Then he got up and said, " You'd better go down to the dugout."

MRS PRESTON (*rising; bewildered*). What dugout?

PEGGY. I don't know. We never had a dugout. We just used the cellar in the War. Mr Preston never used it and didn't even know about it, but it made us see what had happened. We knew he was an air-raid warden in the War, and he suddenly thought it was still on. We talked to him and said it was all right—but he just—kind of mumbled and kept shaking his head. You see—we didn't know *what* to do.

(*There is a slight pause.* MRS PRESTON *is still hostile and profoundly suspicious.*)

MRS PRESTON (*perching herself on the upstage arm of the easy chair* C.). Why didn't you telephone and tell me?

PEGGY. Well—how *could* we? He never told us where he lived and there are crowds of Prestons in the telephone book. Then opening time came. We couldn't have him sitting there in the bar, looking so queer—so my brother Joe took him up to the spare bedroom and made him lie down, hoping he'd get all right. After a while he dozed off. It wasn't an ordinary sleep because we couldn't wake him. When the bar closed at ten we all went up—all three of us—and sat round and talked about what we ought to do.

MRS PRESTON. You could have sent for a doctor.

PEGGY. We *did* think about that. We even thought about the police. He didn't have anything to help us—no identity card or letters or anything—but he was sleeping so quietly, we thought it best to wait and see what happened when he woke up. Joe and I looked in twice during the night. He was still sound asleep. But he woke up quite easily when I took him a cup of tea in the morning. He was still very funny, though. He still didn't seem to know where he lived or the place he worked. He didn't seem to care—or try to think when we asked him.

(*The tired, bewildered brain of* MRS PRESTON *does not take in the significance of all this at first. She is obsessed with suspicion : a belief that the whole thing is a fabrication to explain away some obscure and probably ugly affair as yet concealed. She has no faith in a word of what the woman tells her.*)

He washed, and shaved himself with Joe's razor quite naturally, but his mind was still all mixed up in the War. He kept saying it was a quiet day, with no alarms, but now and then he'd say : " Listen—here's one coming "—or something like that. He was thinking of the fly bombs all the time. We gave him some breakfast and made him stay quiet in his room, but Joe said if he wasn't any better by the evening we'd *have* to tell the police.

MRS PRESTON (*rising*). You knew that his Bank was quite close—why didn't you tell *them*?

PEGGY (*rising ; helplessly*). We didn't know. Of course, we knew he worked in a Bank, but we didn't know where. We never discussed those things and it wasn't our affair.

MRS PRESTON (*moving to* R. *of the stool*). Yes, the doctor said something like that might be possible. What did he do—the whole day?

PEGGY. Well, he just sat about, up there in that bedroom. Soon after five Joe said the only thing to do was to get him quietly round to the police station and tell them what happened. That was really the queerest part of all. I gave him a sherry before Joe took him away—just to set him at his ease. We sat in the saloon bar, and we all had sherry—and all of a sudden he began to change. He looked puzzled and restless and then he sort of braced himself up and said: "Aren't we going to finish our game of darts?" You see? We were sitting round in the same room at the same time of the evening, drinking sherry just like we did the night before. He stood up and took one of the darts and said: "Well, what are we waiting for?" We didn't quite know *what* to do at first—but Joe thought it best not to say a thing about it in case it upset him again. It was kind of uncanny—standing round, playing darts just as if nothing had happened—you know, trying to joke and make ordinary conversation. Then suddenly he said: "Good lord—it's time I went." We didn't like him going off like that alone, but he looked so ordinary and natural when he got his coat and umbrella off the peg that we almost thought *we* were the queer ones. Joe did think perhaps he ought to walk down to . . .

(*She stops abruptly as the door up* C. *opens and* MR PRESTON *enters.*)

MR PRESTON (*at the door up* C.). I've just remembered something, Janet . . .
PEGGY. Oh, hello . . .
MR PRESTON. Why did you come here?
PEGGY. Well, I heard you were in trouble, Dave . . .
MR PRESTON. How did you hear?
PEGGY. A young man who comes from down here said the police had you round yesterday . . .
MR PRESTON (*to* MRS PRESTON). Miss Dobson works with her brother and sister at a place where I drink a glass of sherry on my way to the station in the evening——
PEGGY. Of course, when we read about this awful murder . . .
MR PRESTON. —I should have told you, Janet . . .
MRS PRESTON. Don't worry about that, David. Listen to what Miss Dobson has come to tell you.
PEGGY. I saw at once I'd got to find out where you lived and come down and help you.
MR PRESTON. How can you help me?
MRS PRESTON. Miss Dobson says you spent Monday night at their hotel.
PEGGY. You spent the whole night at *The Feathers*, Dave. Directly I tell them that they can't go after you any more.
MR PRESTON. But I left your place at six o'clock—when St Paul's was striking six.

PEGGY. But that's it—you didn't! I mean, not on the same day as you came in. You didn't come out until this murder was all over.

MR PRESTON. I came into *The Feathers* just after five on Monday evening. It was exactly five by the office clock when I left the Bank. I left your house at six o'clock—while the clock was striking. The police know that.

PEGGY. The police never came near our place—how can they know?

MR PRESTON (*to* PEGGY). Because I told them. Everything I remembered, just as it happened. (*To* MRS PRESTON.) I came down to tell you something, Janet. It all happened in the train coming home. Up in my room, just now, I suddenly remembered quite clearly the people in the compartment when the train left Cannon Street. There was an old man with a flower in his button-hole, and two girls—two girls reading books.

PEGGY. Look, Dave, I know what I'm talking about, and you've got the whole thing mixed up.

MR PRESTON. But later on they were entirely different people. There was a soldier with a haversack and a boy with a parcel. It was a different train. The doctor said that might have happened—I may have got out of the train before it got to Bromley.

PEGGY. How can you leave a train when you aren't even on it? It doesn't matter what you say or think—directly I've been and told the police, your worries are over.

MR PRESTON. Do the police know that you've come here?

PEGGY. Not yet. But they jolly soon will.

MR PRESTON. You know what it would mean if you went to them—how serious it would be? (*He perches himself on the upstage arm of the easy chair* C. *and faces* PEGGY.) You're not a child, Peggy. You realize the consequences?

PEGGY. You don't understand what's happened to you, Dave, and you're not trying to understand.

MR PRESTON. Oh, I am trying, Peggy. I'm trying to understand why these terrible things should happen to me. In the old days they believed in evil spirits that lay in wait for people and suddenly possessed them. What could have made me think that I could save myself by dragging in my best friend and trying to make him stand by me and swear that I was in his house that night? The police would have found him out and arrested him; and that's what would happen to you. (*He rises.*) I want you to go home, now, because you are playing with dangerous things, Peggy. More dangerous than you know. Promise me you'll go home.

PEGGY. I don't know what's come over you, Dave.

MR PRESTON. You promise me?

PEGGY. If that's what you want.

MR PRESTON. I don't mean that I'm not grateful to you.

You came down to help me—and you have helped me—more than I can ever say. I shall always think . . .

(*There is a ring at the front-door bell.* MR PRESTON *exits up* C. *and goes quietly upstairs.* MRS PRESTON *exits up* C. *and opens the front door.* PEGGY *moves to* R. *of the stool.*)

MRS PRESTON. Good evening, Inspector. Will you come in?

(*The* INSPECTOR *comes into the entrance hall.* MRS PRESTON *closes the front door.*)

INSPECTOR. Good evening, Mrs Preston. Is your husband at home?

(*He enters and moves to the fireplace.*)

MRS PRESTON (*up* C.). He's upstairs—but I want you to hear what this young lady has to say. (*She closes the door up* C.)

INSPECTOR (*to* PEGGY). Ah, I expect you're Miss Dobson. I heard you'd come down. I've been having a talk with your brother and sister at *The Feathers* this afternoon.

PEGGY. Oh, you have, have you?

(MRS PRESTON *perches herself on the* L. *arm of the sofa.*)

INSPECTOR. Mr Preston told us yesterday he called in at *The Feathers* that night, but you know he was so definite about leaving at six o'clock that it rather put us off the track at first. Well, Mrs Preston, I'm sure it must be a relief to you. We never really thought he was involved. The thing that had been puzzling us was the coincidence of someone trying to plant a robbery on a man the very night he's missing from home. As a matter of fact it was Mr Preston who helped us there—when he mentioned the little fellow who worked at the hospital in the evenings and the Club kitchen at week-ends. I saw something in that because the hospital knew he was missing at nine o'clock and the Club safe got robbed at ten. We've got a few things to clear up, but as far as Mr Preston's concerned there's nothing more to worry about—it's perfectly all right.

PEGGY (*moving above the easy chair* C.). Oh—so it's perfectly all right, is it? You think you can walk in here smiling and everything *is* all right. Anybody'd think you were talking about a lost dog that's come home. Don't you realize you've made him ill? When you knew he hadn't done it why couldn't you call up from *The Feathers* and tell him? No. Not you. You come sailing back in your own good time. Let him wait, let him suffer. What do his feelings matter? All you fellows are good for is hanging round our place at night—seeing nobody has a glass of beer at five past ten. I'll go now, Mrs Preston. You don't want me about. I do hope he'll be all right. Good night.

MRS PRESTON (*rising*). Good night, and thank you so much for coming down.

(MRS PRESTON *goes into the entrance hall and opens the front door for* PEGGY.)

PEGGY (*in the doorway; to the* INSPECTOR). D'you want me for anything else?

INSPECTOR. No, there's nothing, thank you.

PEGGY. Well, you know where to find me if you do. It's Peggy Dobson, *The Feathers*, River Lane.

(*She goes into the entrance hall and exits by the front door. The* INSPECTOR *crosses to* R. *of the stool.* MRS PRESTON *closes the front door and then starts to go upstairs. She changes her mind, enters the room and closes the door.*)

MRS PRESTON. Inspector, I want to make you understand. For two days and two nights my husband's believed he was a criminal lunatic—waiting to be taken away and locked up for life. Don't you realize what that's done to him?

INSPECTOR. I do, Mrs Preston. I only wish it could have been avoided.

MRS PRESTON (*moving up* L.C.). He's always lived so quietly. He only wanted to do his work, and enjoy his evenings and be happy with his friends. A thing like this—it's nearly driven him mad. He wouldn't even listen to what Miss Dobson had to say. You've got to convince him. I want you to go up and tell him.

INSPECTOR (*crossing to the door up* C.). Of course, Mrs Preston, I'll do whatever I can. (*He opens the door.*) That's why I came. (*He goes into the entrance hall, but re-enters immediately.*) He's coming down.

(MRS PRESTON *closes the window curtains.* MR PRESTON *comes downstairs and into the room. He wears his overcoat and carries his hat.*)

MR PRESTON (*above the easy chair* C.; *facing up stage*). Well—Inspector?

INSPECTOR (L. *of the door up* C.). Well, Mr Preston, I was just coming up to tell you that there's nothing more for you to worry about. I did tell you that yesterday, but in a case like this we've just got to get things clear. You do realize it was you that put us on the right track when you mentioned the little fellow who worked in the Club kitchen and did odd jobs at the hospital? It looks to me as if your Club Steward Robinson and this little chap had planned to get this money maybe Monday night—maybe the next—I don't know. And when they hear the Club Treasurer is missing—well, it's a gift. They break open the safe and share the money, and Robinson goes round to Major Watson and tries to plant it on you. After that it looks like the old story of thieves falling out. Robinson gets a knock over the head and the other chap takes the lot. They picked him up this evening over in Croydon—the money as well, all but a few pounds. I'm afraid it's given you a lot of trouble and anxiety, Mr Preston—but you know it's one of those things that might happen to anybody. We may need your evidence later on, but that's all. I'll send a man round this evening with your bag and suit—oh (*he takes a pair of gloves and a handkerchief from his pocket*), and here's a handkerchief and a pair of gloves you left in the spare room at *The Feathers*. (*He hands the gloves and handkerchief to* MR PRESTON.) I think your solicitor was a bit worried about those. Well, I'll say good night, Mr Preston.

MR PRESTON. I'll see you out.

INSPECTOR. Thank you. Good night, Mrs Preston. Good night.

(*He exits by the front door.* MR PRESTON *sees him out and closes the front door. The telephone rings.* MRS PRESTON *lifts the receiver.*)

MRS PRESTON (*into the telephone*). Hello? . . . Yes, it's Mrs Preston speaking . . .

(MR PRESTON *re-enters the room.*)

No—I don't think he can come now—later on, perhaps . . . Well, wait just a moment. (*She turns to* MR PRESTON.) It's Major Watson. You don't want to speak to him, David, do you?

MR PRESTON (*moving to the desk and taking the receiver from* MRS PRESTON). Yes, I'll speak to Major Watson. (*Into the telephone.*) Good evening, Major Watson . . . Yes, it's good news —I've just been told . . . Why, of course, Major, I knew you never thought that . . . Yes, by all means draw the horses— why not? . . .

(MRS PRESTON *moves to the coffee table and picks up the tray of tea things.*)

Eight o'clock tomorrow evening? I'll be there. . . . Yes, I'll bring the books . . . Good night. (*He replaces the receiver and crosses slowly to the fireplace.*)

MRS PRESTON (*moving with the tray to the door up* C.). You didn't drink your tea, David. It's cold—I'll make some more.

(MR PRESTON *stands by the fireplace, with his back half-turned to* MRS PRESTON.)

Tomorrow you must put the tulips in—and in the afternoon we'll go for a walk in the park. David, it's so wonderful— you're home.

(*She exits up* C. *to the kitchen.*)

MR PRESTON. You've had a terrible time, Janet. I'm afraid I didn't do very much to help. (*He turns.*) I'm going to try . . .

His voice dies away as he sees MRS PRESTON *has gone. The clock strikes seven.* MR PRESTON *turns again to the fireplace, sees the letter on the mantelpiece, picks it up and tears it in pieces as—*

the CURTAIN *falls.*

FURNITURE AND PROPERTY LIST

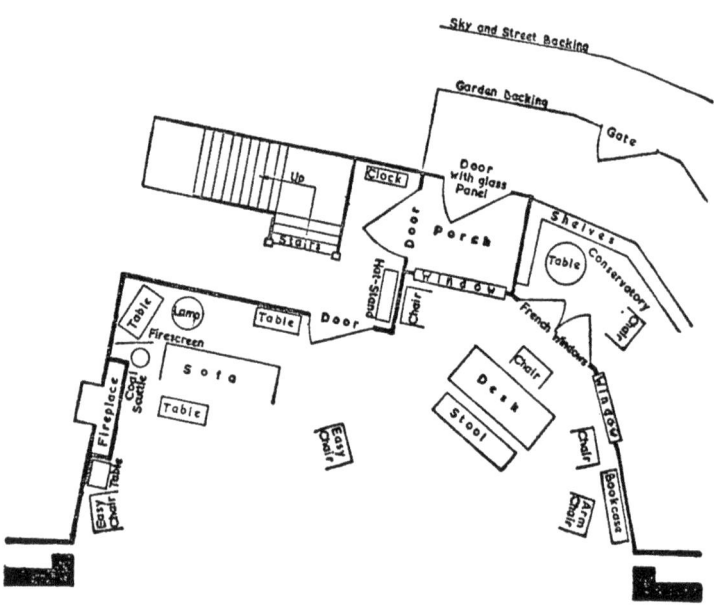

Throughout the play:

On Stage.—Sofa. *On it :* Cushions.
    2 easy chairs. *On them :* Cushions.
    Low coffee table.
    Occasional table (down R.). *On it :* Table-lamp.
    Occasional table (up R.C.). *On it :* Vase of flowers.
    Table (up R.). *On it :* Wireless receiver, vase of flowers, magazines.
    Fender.
    Fire-irons.
    Coal scuttle.
    Fire-screen.
    Hearth-rug.
    On mantelpiece : Vases, ornaments, ashtray, clock.
    Over mantel : Mirror.
    Standard lamp.
    Fireside stool.
    Desk armchair.
    2 dining chairs.
    Desk. *On it :* Telephone, desk-lamp, blotter, inkstand, pens, account books, ashtray.
    Rug under desk.

HOME AT SEVEN

Small armchair.
Bookcase. *On it:* Vase of flowers, telephone directories.
  In it: Books.
Curtains at windows.
Carpet on floor.
4 pairs electric-candle wall-brackets.
Pictures on walls.
Light switches R. of the door up C.
Pipe-rack with pipes on wall below fireplace.

In Entrance Hall.—Grandfather clock.
  Coat-rack.
  Umbrella stand.
  Carpet on stairs.
  Pictures on wall.

In Porch.—Electric pendant with lantern shade.

In Conservatory.—Shelves with dwarf chrysanthemums in pots.
  Wicker table.
  Wicker chair.

Front door fitted with Yale lock.

ACT I

SCENE 1

Set.—*On stool below desk :* Telephone, copy of *The Times*, copy of *Amateur Gardening*.
  On sofa : Rug.
  On coffee table : Tray. *On it :* Teapot, milk jug, sugar basin, cup and saucer.

The fire is alight throughout the play.

Personal.—MRS PRESTON : Handkerchief.
  MR PRESTON : Bunch of keys on chain, umbrella, evening paper.

SCENE 2

Off Stage.—Medical bag. *In it :* Note-book (DR SPARLING).
  Tray. *On it :* Pot of coffee, jug of milk, basin of sugar, cup, saucer, spoon (MRS PRESTON).

Personal.—DR SPARLING : Pencil.

ACT II

SCENE 1

Tidy newspapers on to stool.
Open window curtains.
Off Stage.—Bunch of chrysanthemums (MRS PRESTON).
Personal.—INSPECTOR : Note-book, pencil.

SCENE 2

Off Stage.—Brief-case. *In it :* Papers (SOLICITOR).
  Suitcase (INSPECTOR).

Personal.—SOLICITOR : Pencil.
  DOCTOR : Packet of cigarettes.
  MAJOR : Hat and scarf, matches.
  MR PRESTON : Bunch of keys on chain.

ACT III

Set.—*In fire grate :* Electric kettle with boiling water.
On coffee table : Tray. *On it :* Teapot with tea, tea-cosy, jug with milk, basin with sugar, plate of toast under silver cover, two each cups, saucers, teaspoons.
On desk : Cheque book, sealed letter, small account book, papers.

Turn easy chair c. to face down R.

Off Stage.—Gloves and handkerchief (INSPECTOR).

LIGHTING PLOT

ACT I

Scene 1 (an autumn evening)

To Open.—All lights at ¼.

Standard lamp ⎫
Table-lamp ⎬ off.
Desk-lamp ⎪
Wall-brackets ⎭

Fire on.
Street lamp on.
Porch light off.
Sunset outside window.

Cue 1.—Mr Preston switches on standard lamp—all lights R. up to ½.

Cue 2.—Mr Preston switches on table-lamp—all lights R. up to ¾. Start slow fade of lights outside window (3 minutes).

Cue 3.—Mrs Preston switches on desk-lamp—all lights L. up to ½.

Scene 2 (evening)

To Open.—All lights full up.

Standard lamp ⎫
Table-lamp ⎬ on.
Desk-lamp ⎪
Wall-brackets ⎭

Fire on.
Street lamp on.
Porch light off.
Blue outside windows.

No cues.

ACT II

Scene 1 (morning)

To Open.—All lights full up.

Standard lamp ⎫
Table-lamp ⎬ off.
Desk-lamp ⎪
Wall-brackets ⎭

Fire on.
Street lamp off.
Porch light off.
Bright sunshine outside window.

No cues.

Scene 2 (morning)

Same as Act II, Scene 1
No cues.

ACT III (evening)

To Open.—All lights L. full up.
All lights R. at ¾.
Standard lamp on.
Table-lamp off.
Desk-lamp on.
Wall-brackets on.
Fire on.
Street lamp on.
Porch light off.
Blue outside windows.

Cue 1.—Mr Preston switches off desk-lamp—all lights L. checked to ½.

Cue 2.—Mrs Preston switches on porch light.

Cue 3.—Mrs Preston switches on table-lamp—all lights R. up to full.

www.ingramcontent.com/pod-product-compliance
Ingram Content Group UK Ltd.
Pitfield, Milton Keynes, MK11 3LW, UK
UKHW021845210426
5322IPUK00022B/479